the Healthy Homemade

Pet Food

Cookbook

75

Whole-Food Recipes and
Tasty Treats for Every Age and Stage
of Your Pet's Development

Barbara Taylor-Laino

Foreword by Kenneth D. Fischer, D.V.M.

FAIR WINDS
PRESS
BEVERLY, MASSACHUSETTS

© 2013 Fair Winds Press
Text © 2013 Barbara Taylor-Laino

First published in the USA in 2013 by
Fair Winds Press, a member of
Quayside Publishing Group
100 Cummings Center
Suite 406-L
Beverly, MA 01915-6101
www.fairwindspress.com
Visit www.QuarrySPOON.com and help us celebrate
food and culture one spoonful at a time!

10 9 8 7 6 5 4 3 2 1

ISBN: 978-1-59233-571-8
Digital edition published in 2013
eISBN: 978-1-61058-886-7

Library of Congress Cataloging-in-Publication Data available

Cover and book design: Kathie Alexander
Developmental editor: Jennifer Bright Reich
All photography by Glenn Scott, with food styling by Jessica Weather-
head, with the exception of the following: Cover: top, middle & right;
bottom, middle; gettyimages.com; bottom, left, Shutterstock.com; back
jacket, gettyimages.com, Winnie Au/gettyimages.com, 31; © Nano Calvo/
agefotostock.com, 6; Michael Honor/gettyimages.com, 46; iStockphoto.
com; 19; 29; 30; 66; 84; Clive Nichols/gettyimages.com, 71; Howard Rice/
gettyimages.com, 76; Shutterstock.com; 9; 11; 15; 20; 25; 26; 32; 38; 44; 48;
54; 57; 86; Ulrike Welsch/gettyimages.com, 12; Yellow Dog Productions/
gettyimages.com, 78

Printed and bound in China

The information in this book is for educational purposes only. It is not intended to
replace the advice of a physician or medical practitioner. Please see your health
care provider before beginning any new health program.

Contents

4   **Foreword**
7   **Introduction**

CHAPTER 1
The Pluses to Making Homemade Pet Food | 9

10   Why Fresh Is Best
14   Organic Is Optional
14   Conscious Food Prep

CHAPTER 2
Variety Is the Spice of Health! | 17

18   A Balancing Act
22   All about Meals

CHAPTER 3
The Best Foods for Your Pet | 27

28   Personalizing Your Pet's Meals
38   Age Considerations
41   All or Nothing? Combining Homemade and Commercial Foods

CHAPTER 4
Essential Building Blocks | 45

46   Meats
50   Fats
53   Bones and Calcium
56   Organ Meats
58   Eggs
59   Seeds: Legumes, Nuts, and Grains
61   Vegetables and Fruits
63   Dark, Leafy Greens
64   Fiber or Roughage
65   Dairy

CHAPTER 5
Fine-Tuning Your Homemade Meal Plan | 67

68   Species-Appropriate Super Foods
72   Essential Nutrients
74   Foods to Avoid

CHAPTER 6
Switching to a Homemade Diet | 79

80   Kitchen Readiness
81   Freezing
81   Plating It Up: Serving Suggestions
83   Keeping it Safe and Clean
84   Making the Switch

CHAPTER 7
Healthy Homemade Recipes | 87

88   Getting Started
160   Healthy Snacks and Treats

168   **Appendix 1: Foods That Are Particularly High in Specific Nutrients**
170   **Appendix 2: Some Favorite High-Quality Commercial Food Brands (If You Cannot Make Your Own Pet Food)**
172   **Acknowledgments**

Foreword

As an integrative veterinarian, my goal is to combine the best of both worlds to provide the best care for a patient: conventional Western medicine and complementary, or alternative, medicine. I believe that this combination is what constitutes a truly holistic approach. Regardless of the type of health care a pet receives, the foundation for good health begins with good nutrition. A fundamental component of my initial visit with a client is an in-depth discussion of proper nutrition. I say proper nutrition because all too often, this topic is either ignored completely, or, dare I say it, approached incorrectly by conventional veterinarians. Most veterinarians do not really discuss nutrition with their clients. If they do, they unfortunately give the topic short shrift and/or simply give out information that is incorrect. It is not their fault, however. Just as with our colleagues in human medicine, the nutrition education we receive in school is either severely lacking and/or just plain wrong. I find it a sad irony that in the technologically advanced age we live in, for all of the high-powered medicine available to us, we have lost sight of the most fundamental way to maintain, and in many cases, restore good health. We have gotten so far away from nature in how we feed our pets (and ourselves), we have lost our way.

That all sounds kind of depressing, but here's the good news. The book you are about to read is a road map that will take you back on the path that nature intended. As I read through this book, I was impressed with how much information is packed into these pages. If you have some knowledge of holistic nutrition for pets, this book will help strengthen that knowledge and give you the tools to take it to the next level. If this is your first foray into this wonderful world, then I encourage you to "sit back, relax, and enjoy the ride." If this is all new to you, the challenge is to not become overwhelmed. Barbara Taylor-Laino has provided a smorgasbord of information (pardon the pun), from which you can pick and choose. You may need some time to digest (again, pardon the pun) the information presented before making big changes in your pet-feeding routine. Or, you may dive right in from the start. I have found that over time, many pet owners make the transition from absentmindedly feeding whatever food they happened to pick off the shelf (often whatever was on sale) to thoughtfully providing healthy, balanced meals for their pets. Often, they start off taking baby steps; that's okay. What is important is being more conscious about what you feed your pet and how you do it. By the way, I find that when a pet owner becomes more tuned in to their pet's nutritional needs, it is not uncommon for them to become more aware of their own, so this really becomes a win-win proposition.

I think a note about expense is important here. Better food will cost more to feed your pet than a bargain basement brand.

As Barbara points out, however, compared with a lot of foods that owners already feed their pets, the cost of home-prepared food is not much higher. More important, this way of feeding is the single most important thing you can do to ensure your pet's health. I love seeing my patients for well-care exams once or twice a year. What I do not enjoy is seeing them every month for the recurrent allergy problems (and other chronic problems) that require repeated office visits and medications to control symptoms that would otherwise not be present (or would be much reduced) if they were on healthier diets. I would rather see you spend your pet's health care dollars on his/her nutrition than on office visits and medications that might otherwise be avoided or minimized.

There is a quote by Thomas Edison that is well known in holistic medicine circles: "The doctor of the future will give no medicine, but will instruct his patient in the care of the human frame, in diet, and in the cause and prevention of disease." Although Edison said this about human beings, it applies just as much to our pets.

I am honored that Barbara asked me to write the foreword to this book. Barbara "walks the walk" when it comes to holistic living. When she talks about the love and intent that goes into preparing her pets' meals, she captures a very important essence of what holism is all about.

If I had written a book about this subject, I would have wanted it to be just like this. It wouldn't have, however, because quite honestly, I would not have been able to do it the justice that Barbara has. Her expertise in the kitchen and knowledge of how to put it all together takes the guesswork out of the process for you.

It is my sincere hope that you will incorporate the information in these pages into your life with your pets. You will be better off for it, but most important, your pets will be better off for it. For that, I thank Barbara Taylor-Laino for furthering the cause of holistic pet nutrition on behalf of the pets that will benefit from this knowledge.

Kenneth D. Fischer, D.V.M.

Introduction

On our farm in New York state, we believe in sustainability and natural rearing. Our farm philosophy is to create an environment that supports itself. Our soil, plants, and animals are all cared for and supported naturally. Our original purpose for farming was to provide ourselves and our cats and dogs with great-tasting, fresh, whole, chemical-free food. But it has become so much more—we're not just using the farm, but becoming a part of the living entity that *is* the farm.

Before we moved to the farm, my husband and I lived in an apartment with an Alaskan Malamute puppy named Roara who developed many health issues. We were feeding her a popular, very expensive puppy kibble, but after many visits to veterinarians, she was diagnosed with irritable bowel syndrome, allergies, hot spots, and separation anxiety. This just wasn't what a six-month-old dog's life was supposed to be like.

I started researching pet food, and at the same time, I started my studies, both personally and professionally, in integrative and holistic health and nutrition. I created meal plans for Roara using Juliette de Baïracli Levy, Kymythy Schultze, Wendy Volhard, and Richard Pitcairn as my guides and inspiration. Within a week and a half on a homemade diet, Roara's irritable bowel syndrome calmed down dramatically. Within a month, she had no signs of any digestive disorder, and no more allergies or hot spots. Within three months, her separation anxiety was also showing dramatic improvement.

Although our cat, Sham, had not been having health issues, we realized that after we began feeding her a homemade diet, she was behaving more playfully and had more energy, and her fur was shinier and more brightly striped. Plus, she was definitely enjoying the new food, helping herself to steamed broccoli florets and chicken hearts and purring while eating them.

Shortly afterward, we took in another dog and completely filled the apartment patio with potted plants. We realized it was time to move to a place with more room. Fifteen years later, we are running a certified organic CSA (Community-Supported Agriculture) and herb farm. What had been a diet and meal plan for our cats and dogs turned into a way of life for all of us. Now I plan and make the animal food right along with the people food each day, using whole, seasonal, fresh ingredients—organic meats, fats, grains, nuts, vegetables, herbs, and greens. It works beautifully. It feels right.

Making your own pet food will involve a bit more time and planning on your part than it takes to simply buy a bag of commercial pet food. Instead, you'll be including your pet's food needs on your own shopping list. In the kitchen, you'll have to make time to mix up and cook the pet food along with the human food. And for the first few weeks, you'll be experimenting—figuring out what your pet likes, what types of meals integrate easily into your household routine, and so on. But the process will soon feel natural and comfortable. You'll find that you can actually save money by using better-quality ingredients because the food portions will be smaller. You'll see your pet thriving, interacting with the kitchen activities, and thoroughly enjoying the variety of meals. Equally important, most people who start to feed their pets healthy, homemade food end up making healthier food choices for themselves as well!

 **CHAPTER 1**

The Pluses to Making Homemade Pet Food

Diet is the foundation for vibrant health for people and pets. Along with providing a happy lifestyle with exercise, clean water, and love, a diet of fresh, whole foods homemade by you is the best thing you can do for your pet.

There is currently an epidemic of poor food choices in our society. We're over-dependent on quick and easy, processed, premade foods in our own and our pets' diets. We're feeding our pets commercialized foods with many ingredients (such as sugars, colors, and salt) that are there solely for marketing reasons rather than for providing nourishment. We have been led away from the kitchen, and it is becoming clear that this way of nourishing our pets and ourselves simply doesn't work in the long run.

Why Fresh Is Best

When you use whole, fresh foods, you are building meals using high-quality ingredients that are fresh and alive. By making your own homemade pet food, you are assuring that your cat or dog gets the healthiest food for supporting vibrant health.

Cats, Dogs, and the Foods They Naturally Love

Different species of animals have different metabolisms and digestive systems. Each type of animal has evolved to eat particular foods and can best absorb the nutrients from those foods. If the animal is suddenly exposed to a new food or to a food that isn't right for that particular animal, there is a good chance that the nutrients will not be able to be digested fully or appropriately. In short, the food has to match the digestive system of the species. In order to get an idea of what foods would best match the digestive systems of cats and dogs, we need to look at the natural diet of their wild counterparts.

Cats are true, hard-core carnivores. They eat mostly meat, and it really needs to be as fresh as possible for them to fully absorb its nutrients. Meat is best for cats when it is still warm after they hunt it down and kill it. They eat the whole carcass of whatever small animal they catch—they need nutrients from all parts of the animal. Cats can also abosrb quite a few important nutrients from vegetable matter and dairy, but what the vegetable matter is paired with makes a big difference. The domestic cat has spent a lot of generations with humans and has gotten used to being a part of the household and being fed with kitchen scraps along with the prey they catch.

Dogs are more like humans—they are omnivores. The digestive system of dogs can absorb nutrition from a wide range of whole foods, such as meat, grain, dairy, and vegetable matter. Most dogs do need higher protein levels than humans, and dogs also are scavengers, so they can obtain nutrients from not-so-fresh meat. Dogs have spent thousands of years with humans and have adapted to being able to eat and be sustained by much human food.

It's important to remember that as great as certain ingredients may sound, if they are not foods that are matched to the species you're feeding, then they are worthless at best or can even be detrimental, so it is crucial to always keep species appropriateness in mind. A wide variety of whole, fresh foods that are suitable for cats and dogs will be discussed in upcoming chapters.

Same Meal Every Day?

When you make your own pet food, you are completely in charge of what your pet eats. You can provide a bountiful variety of ingredients and meal types throughout the week and month. This variation is what balances the food nutritionally for your pet. You will hear people say that it is hard to balance a meal for a cat or dog. What they mean is that it is hard to make sure that each meal has exactly the right amount of nutrients deemed necessary by organizations such as the AAFCO (The Association of Animal Feed Control Officials). Indeed, that's true. But that's not your goal. If you were feeding the same exact meal every day, yes, it would be extremely important that it at least had the minimum nutrient requirements as recommended by the AAFCO. But that is not what you're doing when you are preparing homemade meals for your pets. And these generalized standards are never holistic in essence and are always oversimplified. They don't have the ability to take into account sources for foods and level of nutrients; empty, poor-quality calories are counted the same as high-quality calories. They give a quantity for ideal protein, but don't take into account the quality of protein or the ability of your pet to absorb that protein source. Besides, you don't want to provide minimum nutrient requirements—you want to provide the full array of nutrients necessary for thriving, vibrant animals! You don't need to be a chemist, or try to decide whether some new highly processed additive is detrimental or not. Putting your trust in whole food sources and foods produced as naturally and sustainably as possible is a smart approach to pet nutrition.

Six Reasons Why Homemade Is Better

1. Cleanliness. Even the most high-quality, commercially produced food is still mass-produced. The manufacturer is not, for example, cutting out the little mushy spots on the carrots that you would cut out when preparing your own. When you make your own pet food, you know you won't have to ever worry about pet food recalls.

2. Cost. Pet food costs have been rising and those of the organic super-premium brands have increased dramatically recently. You can save close to 50 percent per serving with careful shopping and buying in bulk.

3. Intention. When you make your own meals for your pet, you are adding your loving and good intentions to the food as you mix, chop, prepare, and serve them.

4. Freshness. Homemade pet food just tastes better—and has more nutrients, antioxidants, and essential fatty acids than commercially prepared versions, simply due to fresh ingredients.

5. Quality. You can choose the level of quality that matches your budget as well as the availability of foods you have in your area and are in-season. And you can make choices: Maybe you will not be able to afford the organic eggs one month, but for the other months of the year you can, so your pets are still getting that benefit.

6. Control. Last but not least, you have total control—if your pet is allergic to certain ingredients, you won't include them. You can make foods that match your individual pet's needs and likes.

Organic Is Optimal

Organic vegetables are raised without chemical fertilizers or poisonous pesticides and herbicides, and are therefore much better tolerated and metabolized by both humans and animals.

Although cats and dogs can eat food chemicals and pesticides and not get sick immediately, it doesn't mean we should feed them food laced with these poisons! While a pesticide is designed to effectively kill a small bug and not harm us, remember that our pets are smaller than us, and can be expected to be more negatively affected by exposure to pesticides than we are.

When it comes to feeding your pet meats, look for those that are labeled "grass-fed." Poultry should be labeled "pasture-raised" to assure they were raised with access to an outside field. Buying "certified organic" meats ensures not only the lack of antibiotics and hormones, but also guarantees that the animals weren't fed GMOs (genetically modified organisms). Why be so picky? Because meat of grass-fed and pasture-raised animals that are raised humanely, in sunlight and with exercise, translates into good, healthful meat. One example of this goodness is vitamin D; pets can get perfect, readily absorbed vitamin D from meat, but only from meat raised in sunlight (grass-fed or pasture-raised meat).

The meat of a grass-fed animal also has the proper vegetable presence in it. If the animal did not have access to grass, then your cat or dog won't get this vegetable component. This vegetable presence is absorbed differently by cats and dogs than are actual vegetables added to the meal.

Conscious Food Prep

It feels good to prepare meals from sustainable, ethical ingredients. You're doing a wonderful thing for your pet by preparing his or her food in your kitchen. Enjoy the experience as it happens—don't rush through it or feel overwhelmed. As you prepare your pet's meals, keep your mind and intentions on promoting and encouraging vibrant health and active, glowing energy. The expectations you have for your pet have so much to do with his or her health and enjoyment of the food you lovingly prepare.

Of course, making your own homemade pet food means taking on work and responsibility. You will be in charge of making sure your pet gets all the nutrients he or she needs. It will also take some planning and time management. But it will be worth it. I hope that the recipes and ideas in this book will help you feel confident and inspired, as well as empowered and organized.

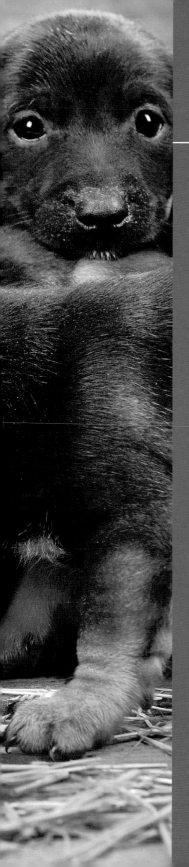

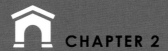 **CHAPTER 2**

Variety Is the Spice of Health!

You are not going to feed your cat or dog the same meal every day.

For many people, this is a huge, fundamental change in thinking. The idea that feeding the same meal each day is "normal" is a major part of the marketing plan for the commercial pet food industry. But the idea of feeding the same meal every day reminds me of those futuristic science fiction stories in which humans survive on nutrient pills that contain the daily allowance of nutrients in a single swallow. It can never work. Although the pet food industry has come up with a general guideline of necessary daily nutrients that may keep most cats and dogs alive, vibrant health just won't be possible for most pets fed that way. Simply put, your pet cannot thrive on the same food every day.

A Balancing Act

The pet food industry has made the question of how to balance your cat's or dog's meal into a dramatic—even traumatic— problem. But here's the key: It is not the meal you need to balance; it's the diet that needs to be balanced. By diet, I mean everything your pet eats, taking into account the daily food, the weekly food, the monthly food, and the food throughout your pet's lifetime. It is silly to try to perfectly balance each meal according to an oversimplistic and very possibly wrong set of criteria. Instead, you should be providing a variety of meals using a wide range of whole, fresh ingredients that intrinsically provide your pet with balanced and vibrant health.

The recipes in chapter 7 need to be mixed and matched and built upon as inspiration for your own recipes. Don't just pick one of these recipes and make it every day for your pet. Your pet will not be getting a balanced diet that way. The recipes are labeled with categories that will help you organize them and make sure you are providing variety.

Mix It Up

How do you go about providing variety in your pet's meals? You need to consider meat and protein sources, dairy, greens, and grains. You will also be able to provide variety by mixing up the way you pair different foods and prepare the meals. Here's a brief overview of the approach to take; you'll find more detailed meal how-to in chapters 4 and 5.

- **Meat and protein sources.** You want to use a variety of meats, and beef and chicken are probably the two that are easiest to find. But you should also consider fish, turkey, lamb, goat, and game animals. Fish can be bought fresh or frozen. Canned fish is also a healthy option; wild-caught pink Alaskan salmon, jack mackerel, and sardines are all good choices. Nutrient-rich shellfish can also be considered. Turkey is a great meat to feed your pets and can be naturally calming. High-quality meat is key here, though: Don't feed your pet Thanksgiving leftovers such as skin and gristle or highly fatty gravy. Cornish game hens are nice and small and match the size of the natural wild prey of many of our pets. Lamb and goat are good, healthy meats and can provide protein when pets exhibit allergies to the more typical meat sources. Sometimes the most inexpensive and natural meat can be in the form of venison and rabbit, both of which are wonderful foods for cats and dogs. Don't be afraid to be creative when seeking out meat sources.

- **Dairy and eggs.** Eggs are fabulous additions to your pet's meals, providing protein and a generous variety of nutrients. And dairy products such as butter, cheese, and yogurt are great to use in small amounts to provide extra variety.

- **Greens and grains.** When thinking about pet food, many people overlook the vast variety of vegetable foods—including nuts, seeds, grains, leafy greens, herbs, vegetables, and fruits. These whole foods make a welcome addition to a balanced pet diet.

When you focus on fresh, whole foods for your pet, you can buy seasonally and locally. This allows you to take advantage of sales and other buying opportunities, and it lets you be creative in the kitchen.

How you prepare your pet's food also helps provide variety. You can serve some meals raw, others cooked, and others can be a combination of the two. You can also serve some meals with grains and others completely grainless. You'll probably find yourself doing a lot of experimenting at first as you get used to preparing the diet and your pet shows you what he or she likes or dislikes. Whatever you do, don't let yourself get into a rut—keep up the creativity and stay open to variety.

Cooked versus Raw

Raw meat is what the wild counterparts to our cats and dogs eat and thrive on. The digestive systems of cats and dogs are designed for eating raw meat and absorbing all the nutrients they need from it. Once we start cooking and processing it, the meat becomes less nutritious. This doesn't mean that a cat or dog won't be able to get any nutrition from cooked meat, just not the most they could be getting. A wild puma or coyote might not do so well if fed cooked human food, but many domestic cats and dogs can actually be quite healthy on a cooked diet. Then again, many cats and dogs could do much better on a raw diet, and some may need a raw diet in order to thrive. For others, a raw diet may not work at all. Keep in mind that even if you cook all of your pet's food, you are still providing a diet far above and beyond what your pet would get out of a bag of commercial kibble. The amount of raw meat you include in your pet's food is completely up to you.

When I am making pet food, I usually focus on raw meals. But my pets also share many of our human meals. I also take advantage of a lot of cooked "super foods" such as canned salmon and sardines.

Just be aware that cats' and dogs' digestive systems probably won't be able to absorb as much nutrition from cooked meat as they could from raw, so take this into consideration when preparing cooked food and consider including a multivitamin in your pet's diet. Taurine is one example: It is an essential amino acid that cats need, yet it is virtually destroyed in cooked meats. So you must add it as a supplement to your cooked meal.

There is also more moisture content in raw meat, and cats, especially, tend to depend on their food for a great amount of their liquid needs. That's one reason why feeding a cat a diet of dry kibble can lead to urinary tract problems. So be sure the cooked food you serve your pet is adequately moist.

A Note on Safety

Raw meat is quite safe for your cat or dog to eat. Their digestive systems are very different from our own—they are short, fast, and highly acidic. Bacteria simply don't have time to fester and multiply in a healthy cat or dog with a fully functioning immune system. But you do want to be responsible and follow the rules for food handling that you would use for meat you are cooking for yourself. Rinse off meat, keep it cold, and don't use it if it smells bad or if the expiration date has passed. I like to grind my own meat using slightly frozen cuts rather than buying pre-ground; this way I have control over the cleanliness and purity.

All about Meals

As I discussed earlier, there is nothing overly complicated about feeding your pet good, healthy meals. Again, variety is key, and you can introduce variety not only by mixing up ingredients but also by altering meal portions, feeding times, and the number of meals per day.

Meal Size

Carnivores may sometimes catch a mouse for a day's sustenance and other times a fat chicken. On other days, they may find only nuts and berries. So it's not in their nature to eat the same quantity of food day after day. That's why I like changing up the size and nature of my animals' meals, and you should, too.

Feeding Times

Some people feel that it is important to feed their animals at the same time every day. This is not important to carnivores—as hunters, they expect food to come as it may. So don't get hung up on watching the clock and feeding your pet on the dot. This will also free you up from sticking to a strict time schedule for meals.

How Many Meals per Day?

Some cats and dogs do best when fed one meal a day. Most do well on one lighter meal and one heavier meal per day. Some will need three or four small meals. It depends on the individual animal as well as on your schedule. I personally like to do a light meal in the morning and then a larger meal in the evening, but I don't stick to it religiously. Sometimes I skip the breakfast and serve lunch instead.

Basically, feel free to make decisions on timing your pets' meals according to their individual needs and your own schedule. Don't feel forced into some dogmatic routine of when a meal should be served or how often. Trust your instincts and make this work for you. Your pets will do just fine if you skip a meal or serve it at an unusual time, or if you only have time to add some fresh whole food extras to a commercial diet.

Approaches to Fasting

A fast involves a period of not eating, or cutting back drastically on what is eaten. It is often undertaken so the body can take a break from digestion, and detoxify. The digestive systems of cats and dogs are particularly well set up for fasting. Their wild counterparts are carnivore hunters that are often in a position of having to fast because game can be scarce.

Our domestic cats and dogs need these periods of digestive rest in order to be truly healthy. When a meal is skipped, the digestive system can take a break and catch up and clean up. I find that skipping a pet's meal can be helpful for dealing with digestive upsets such as mild diarrhea. When they are not feeling well, some cats and dogs will naturally stop eating. But others will eat the food we put out for them even if they don't really want to, just out of habit. If one of my pets has diarrhea in the morning, I usually skip serving breakfast. By the late afternoon, the diarrhea has usually cleared up, but I keep dinner light, serving a small amount of a mostly meat-based meal.

Scheduling a fast for your pet once a week or a couple of times a month is a good thing. Always provide fresh water on fast days. The type of fast can vary: You can withhold all foods, you can do a day of just broth, you can simply cut back on the size of the regular meals, or if you usually feed mostly meat, your pet's fast day can be a day of mostly grain and dairy. The point is to provide some dramatic variety.

A Sample Week of Meals

Here are some suggestions for a single week of meals using recipes you'll find in chapter 7. Follow this week of meals with completely different ones, depending on local availability, individual preferences, the size of your pet, and so on. Observe and monitor your pet and make adjustments if a food doesn't seem to agree with him or her or if you see weight gain or loss.

SUNDAY

Morning
Sardine Salad; *page 154*

Evening
Zucchini and Eggs; *page 148*

MONDAY

Morning
Barley and Jack Mackerel; *page 134*

Evening
Ground Chicken Dinner with Seasonal Vegetables; *page 90*

TUESDAY

Morning
Purple Berry Meat; *page 122*

Evening
Ground Chicken Dinner with Seasonal Vegetables; *page 90*

WEDNESDAY

Morning
Beef, Sardines, and Polenta; *page 100*

Evening
Turkey with Millet, Fennel, and Tahini; *page 95*

THURSDAY

Morning
Nettle Rice; *page 145*

Evening
Beef, Sardines, and Polenta; *page 100*

FRIDAY

Morning
Ground Turkey with Arugula; *page 121*

Evening
"Essentials" Dinner of Canned Salmon, Egg, and Chicken Hearts; *page 109*

SATURDAY

Morning
Ground Frozen Fish Mash with Seasonal Vegetables; *page 94*

Evening
Big Baked Veggies and Lamb Chunks; *page 115*

CHAPTER 3

The Best Foods for Your Pet

To achieve nutritional balance in your pet's homemade diet, you must provide variety. And the key to planning a variety-rich diet is to take your animal's individuality into account. While commercial food is designed to be universal, your homemade food is designed by you for your specific pet, within your own household culture. There truly is an art to creating meals for your individual cat or dog.

Personalizing Your Pet's Meals

Every animal is an individual, and an ingredient that works for one animal may not agree with another; even littermates can have very different reactions to food. Allergies are one obvious reaction, but there are other, more subtle, reactions to food that should be taken into account as you build your pet's diet. For example, ground chicken may be the perfect protein source for your gentle and slightly lazy cat, seemingly giving her extra energy and a friendlier disposition, but it may lead to extra nervousness and even anxiety in your other, more high-strung, cat. You'll want to consider the individual and personal needs of your specific pet as you create meal plans.

To get started in personalizing your pet's meals, you need to understand your pet's history, personality, eating style, and more. Here's a rundown of what you need to know.

History

Your pet's history is a good starting place for evaluating what your pet's individual diet needs may be. If you bought your kitten or puppy from a caring and responsible breeder and she has been nurtured and pampered all her life, you may not need to worry much about addressing health issues. But you do want to know what the breeder was feeding and if there were any adverse reactions to certain foods. Also, try to find out if the parents of your kitten or puppy are healthy or if the breed itself tends to have certain genetic issues or diseases.

If you are adopting your animal from a shelter, you may not have any real background information available to you. Ask the people at the shelter to tell you as much as they can about the animal you are adopting. Questions about how your new pet interacts with the other animals and how she eats, sleeps, and displays aggression or anxiety will help you make comparisons and allow you to build a historical profile.

Take this background information into consideration when thinking about your pet's mealtimes; food and eating are huge parts of animals' lives and can play a significant role in their emotional and social reactions. For many animals, feeding time may be associated with stress and competition. If you have a multiple-animal household, make sure you are aware of what is happening socially at feeding time, and if you see that one of your pets is becoming stressed, be ready to provide alternative feeding arrangements.

I worked with one client whose mixed-breed dog was experiencing constant diarrhea no matter what types of food we tried. She was the only animal in the household, but she gulped her food and fretted and became snappy if anyone approached her while she was eating. Apparently she had some experience in her background where feeding time was stressful and she couldn't get over it. We decided she needed privacy and reassurance and moved her feeding time out of the busy kitchen and into a small and dimly lit bathroom and closed the door. The human family made sure to be relatively quiet and calm outside the bathroom while she ate. At first she continued the pattern, but after a couple of days, she started feeling comfortable enough to eat more slowly, and the diarrhea started to ease up. A year later, she is now eating back in the kitchen and even sharing with us at the supper table, finally realizing that the stress from her past no longer exists.

If you find that your pet is experiencing stresses derived from the past, consider making some routine changes. For example, if your cat was bullied by other cats in the past while eating, a good change might be to feed each animal in your household in a different room. For genetically linked health issues, talk with your veterinarian—he or she should be able to give you nutritional advice. A holistic or integrative veterinarian can provide detailed nutritional information you can apply to your individual pet.

Food Background

Consider your pet's food background. If your cat has only been fed kibbles or canned, mushy cat food, she may have no idea what to do if you present her with a whole chicken heart. Introduce it gradually—start by grinding or finely chopping the heart; then once she's used to that, start chopping it less and less, slowly working up to serving a whole one. Don't be discouraged if this doesn't work out for your cat. My one cat will never get used to a whole heart; I have to chop it a little or she just bats it across the kitchen floor! Also, you will be introducing all sorts of new flavors that your pet may love eventually, but may be nervous about when first introduced. Be prepared to be patient and creative.

You may find that the transition period to a new, homemade diet lasts longer than you expected. Be aware that if you are switching from a commercial food to a homemade one—particularly from a grain-based, bulky food to a concentrated, mostly meat food—your pet will have to go through a certain amount of adjustment. Your pet may feel cheated if he's used to a big bowl of food and is now presented with a smaller serving of high-quality food. Also, your pet's metabolism may need some time to revamp itself and process the food properly.

You can make the transition easier by taking your time. Don't rush it! You may be excited to start your pet on a new way of healthy eating, but take little steps. Start by adding a couple spoonfuls of new food to your pet's current food. Use simple ingredients with tastes and textures similar to what you've been feeding up until now. You don't want to overwhelm your pet. I know many pets, especially cats, who have become overwhelmed by too many new ingredients at once, were turned off from variety, and became suspicious at mealtime.

Personality

In addition to considering your pet's past events and experiences, you must also take his or her personality into account. Some animals are naturally nervous, while others are overtly friendly and easy-going. Sometimes a trait can seem like a genuine part of your pet's personality but is really a reaction to certain foods. With overhyper dogs, be especially aware of the percentage of carbohydrates in the diet. Often people associate protein in the diet with hyperactivity, but it is usually due to low-quality carbohydrates often found in commercial foods, which break down into sugars too quickly. If your pet has this tendency, you'll want to integrate higher percentages of protein into the diet. High-quality, meat-based protein provides energy, stamina, and well-being to most carnivores. For a dog who appears fatigued and slow, higher-protein food would also provide natural energy. Keep track of the amount of protein and the type of protein, and your pet's reactions to it. You may find that your pet is sluggish after eating a beef-based meal and is vibrant and energetic after eating a chicken-based meal. It is important to always be observing and critically assessing your pet's reaction to the food you're feeding.

Your pet's food can affect his or her mental and emotional states as well. I have seen many animals who were depressed or dealing with separation anxiety make remarkable improvements after they were switched to a homemade diet.

Energy Levels and Exercise

When you switch your pet from a commercial diet to a homemade one, you'll probably notice that your pet is more energetic. Providing regular exercise will not only help your pet burn off some of that energy but will also promote a more efficient and fully functioning metabolism for proper digestion. Animals need exercise to feel at their best emotionally and physically. But some animals don't have the opportunity to get regular exercise, and as they age, they start to slow down more and more. It is important to be aware of how much exercise and energy your animal puts out and adjust his meals accordingly. This will help to prevent weight gain as well as hormonal imbalances.

Eating Style

Your pet's eating style can be very important when choosing meals. For instance, if you have a Labrador retriever who basically inhales his food in one gulp, you should avoid including chunks of bone and whole vegetables in his meals, and instead grind the bones and raw vegetables to promote better digestibility and avoid a choking hazard. Grind chicken necks and other meat pieces that are small enough to be swallowed whole. (Most of the recipe ingredients in this book can be easily ground up.) On the other hand, a Siberian husky who carefully chews and introspectively eats can be allowed such things as bony chunks and whole carrots in his meal because you know you can trust him to chew everything, and this introspective eater will enjoy the variety of textures.

It's important to watch your pet's reaction as you prepare the food and present him with his bowl. Does he start eating before it even leaves your hand? Is the food gone within seconds? Watch his jaws and get a sense of how thoroughly he is chewing. Most animals who eat too fast also don't chew well. Cats and dogs are meant to use the chewing process to clean their teeth and to fully start the digestive processes and metabolism. And finally, check the stool! If you can recognize bits and pieces of what he ate the day before, then you can assume he's not chewing properly, and he's not taking full advantage of all the nutrients in his meals.

Some pets who eat too fast are doing so because they are stressed. In that case, you need to eliminate stresses in the eating environment, such as other pets who might cause a competitive atmosphere. You might also consider changing up the feeding routine to break your pet out of what has simply become the bad habit of gobbling his food. Try feeding a series of smaller meals in a row rather than one big meal.

At the other extreme, some cats and dogs like to browse at their food throughout the day, having a few bites, wandering off, and going back to it later. If your pet is one of these super-slow eaters, make sure you are not feeding too much. Is your animal at optimal weight? Keep in mind that fresh foods do not last as long as a bowl of kibble, so if you find the food is sitting out in the bowl all day, cut back to two half meals, keeping the second half in the fridge until you're ready to serve it.

Breed

Breed is mainly an issue for dog owners. (Although a Persian cat and a Siamese cat may seem quite different, the differences between a dachshund and a Great Pyrenees are much more pronounced.) Certain dog breeds have developed very different responses to food and how they metabolize it. Breeds such as Alaskan Malamutes, raised for centuries on an Arctic diet where zinc is plentiful, have rather restricted zinc metabolisms. Most Alaskan Malamutes will need zinc supplementation to really thrive unless they are fed a diet that includes lots of Arctic elements such as salmon and seaweed. By the same token, it also makes sense that dogs bred over time in hot desert and tropical environments may have trouble fully metabolizing the same food as Northern European hunting dogs. For an ingredient to get metabolized fully and effectively, the body has to recognize the food.

Of course, all dogs are still canines and are very similar genetically, so I wouldn't make the type of breed a huge influence in choosing foods for your dog, but it does feel very right to feed salmon to Malamutes and rabbits to Whippets.

Size

The size of dog can also make a difference in what you are feeding. For example, you wouldn't give a Chihuahua a beef shank bone to chew on. But it is also interesting to consider what size prey the dog would be able to bring down in the wild. This is one reason why many pet nutritionists are against using beef in homemade diets. There are not many breeds of dog that can bring down a steer! And if they did bring down a large animal like that, they would be eating it for a long time—going back to the carcass as it starts to rot and break down. This breaking down provides all sorts of nutrients and enzymes that you can actually integrate into a homemade diet without having to resort to a rotting steer carcass. And keep in mind the history and purpose of the breed. In the example of Chihuahuas, they usually do very well on beef—probably because they were bred for households where they shared people food; this breed was never on its own in the wild.

I like the idea of feeding the meat of smaller animals to my dogs because I believe that in nature, they would have been eating lots of smaller animals. Even wolves eat mostly mouse- and rabbit-size prey.

Unlike dogs, cats are all similar in size and well connected to their original wild roots. Cats will catch and eat things that range in size from bugs to rabbits. Although I watched my neighbor's cat stalking a deer and chasing it, there is no way he could have actually killed it for dinner. The deer wasn't so sure, though!

So while I wonder how good it is to feed large-animal meat like beef to such small predators, I also want to emphasize that every pet is an individual. If you find that beef works well for your pet, then go with it. Dogs and cats have evolved with humans, and beef and other large game has been a staple in human diets and has been shared with household pets for hundreds of years. That is also why I believe dogs and cats can thrive on foods such as dairy, grains, and vegetables that are unavailable to their counterparts in the wild.

A Word about Portion Size

There are many things to take into consideration when determining the amount of food you should be feeding your pet: the size, breed, and build of your pet; whether he or she is spayed or neutered; your pet's activity level; the food quality; your pet's temperament/nervousness level; your pet's age; even the weather and climate. Some foods will have a tendency to make some animals gain weight, and the amount you will need to feed will probably change throughout the course of your pet's life.

The best way to determine the right quantity of food is to observe your pet and become familiar with his weight and structure. Feel along his sides—how do his ribs feel? Some breeds such as greyhounds should have prominent ribs, but for most breeds of cats and dogs, the ribs should be about as prominent as a human's. Are his hip bones sticking out or snugly nestled in the flesh? Next, feel his spine. Can you feel knobbiness? Are the vertebrae protruding dramatically? If you're not sure what a healthy structure should feel like, ask your veterinarian to show you on your own animal. If you familiarize yourself with your pet's body structure, you won't get food amounts wrong. You'll quickly notice if your pet is feeling chubby, and then you can reduce the amount of food or choose foods that are less likely to cause weight gain, and provide more opportunities for your pet to exercise. And, of course, if your pet begins to look too skinny or acts hungry after finishing a meal, you'll know to add a bit more food.

Age Considerations

In general, the nutritional needs of cats and dogs don't change much as they mature. But you will see your pet's food responses changing over time. As a result, your meal planning will be a constantly changing and evolving art, and it's up to you to be observant and reactive.

Kittens and Puppies: Starting Out on the Right Track

Kittens and puppies give you the opportunity to start from the very beginning with an all-natural, clean diet and lifestyle. Although it is never too late to change a cat or dog over to a natural homemade diet, it is nice to be able to give such protection from the very start.

In the wild, baby animals basically eat the same diets as their parents. If your kitten or puppy is old enough to no longer require nursing, you won't need to add extra dairy to the diet. You may need to chop or grind the food up more, though.

Kittens and puppies are impressionable—this is the age when many habits are formed, so be proactive with foods. I put extra effort into exposing kittens and puppies to new foods and ingredients while they are young and open to such things. Keep mealtimes calm and peaceful, add different textures for chewing, and introduce them to bones to start gnawing with their baby teeth. It is important to allow them to become familiar with bones and learn now how to chew them safely, so once their adult teeth and strength come in, you'll be much more confident about giving them whole bones. I believe that one of the main reasons why so many adult dogs tend to splinter and crack bones is because they were not exposed to bones as puppies. They simply don't know how to go about chewing them safely.

I also believe that kittens and puppies should never eat so much in one meal that their sides stick out. It is much healthier to feed a series of small meals than a couple of overly large ones. Keep in mind that your kitten or puppy has just gone through the most stressful period of her life, being separated from her mother, littermates, and original home. The stress may make her seem overly hungry or competitive for food, so, again, I emphasize that it is important to keep everything as peaceful as possible.

Considering all the changes kittens and puppies are going through, I like to add stomach-settling and calming ingredients to their food. Slippery elm bark is an herbal soother for your pet's digestive system, which is undergoing tremendous changes between weaning and joining your household. The smell of it now always reminds me of puppies! Simply mix 2 tablespoons (9 g) of powder into every 2 cups (400 g) of food at least for the first two weeks after you bring your puppy or kitten home. Then you can cut back to 1 tablespoon (4.5 g) for the following two weeks.

I feed kittens and puppies more cooked and mashed vegetable matter rather than raw, ground vegetables. In particular, I feed extra cooked carrots. I also add almond butter to their meals. If you feed grain, put the grain through a food processor for very young kittens and puppies, so the pieces are smaller. You'll have to keep a close eye while cooking these grains, though, because they will cook much faster than whole grains.

Never Too Late: New Energy for Older Pets

As with kittens and puppies, older animals in the wild also don't change their diets as they age.

If you have been feeding your pet a good natural diet, the only major change you may need to make is to cut back on the amount of food if your older animal starts to put on excess weight. You may feel bad about doing so, but do not let your older animals become obese; this is extremely detrimental. As cats and, especially, dogs age, their joints are not as lubricated as when they were younger, and excess weight on the joints can damage and stress them dramatically.

Also, take a good look at the routines of your older pets. Many people and animals fall into a routine over the years, barely realizing that outside exercise time has been cut short. Make an extra effort to ensure your older pet is getting ample and appropriate exercise.

Older animals may have health issues, which can be affected by diet. If so, be sure to work with your veterinarian to design a diet that addresses these issues in a safe way.

It is never too late to transition an older pet to a natural, homemade diet. Work gradually, just as you would with a younger cat or dog. You can make a big difference in your older animal's vitality and liveliness with new foods. Just adding whole, fresh foods to the regular kibble can add a lot of nutrients and variety, and will be interesting and fun for your older pet.

There are some things to consider when switching an older pet from a commercial, kibble-based diet to a new, fresh foods diet. An older cat or dog may take longer to adjust, may be more finicky, and will mostly likely need more time and patience on your part. If you want to feed whole bones, check the teeth of your elderly animal; you may have to grind the bones, depending on how healthy your pet's teeth are.

Consider the addition of probiotics and extra digestive enzymes to aid in the transition. I also feed my older dogs more vitamin C and give a glucosamine and chondroitin supplement with their meals.

Although it may seem a bit stressful to change an older animal over to a new diet, it is worth it. I have seen so many older cats and dogs get a second wind once they have changed to a homemade, natural diet.

All or Nothing? Combining Homemade and Commercial Foods

Don't assume that feeding your pet a homemade diet has to be an all-or-nothing routine. You can make a huge difference in your pet's health by supplementing a good commercial diet with whole-food side dishes. Buy the best-quality ingredients you can afford and focus on nutrient-rich foods. An egg, a scoop of canned fish, a steamed carrot, a dollop of yogurt, or some fresh chicken liver are perfect additions to a meal of commercial food. With very little work and expense, you can really elevate the nutritional level of each meal.

Even small additions to your pet's diet can have big effects healthwise; if your pet has the building blocks of a variety of healthy nutrients in her system, then she will be able to compensate for any unhealthy ingredients or foods. For instance, if your cat has always had a healthy diet and a friend comes over and gives her a commercial cat treat full of horrible preservatives, sugar, and artificial flavors, you don't need to worry. You can feel confident that your cat has the nutritional building blocks in her system to handle the onslaught of the bad food.

Also, by adding fresh ingredients to your pet's commercial food, you won't unbalance anything, despite the claims of the commercial brands' advertising and marketing. But because commercial diets are in general designed to provide a full balance of nutrients in one serving, I would suggest that to be safe, don't add more than 25 percent extra ingredients on a regular basis. For example, if the maker of your commercial food recommends that you feed your golden retriever 2 cups of canned food (400 g) per day, then when you want to add some canned salmon, feed ½ cup (113 g) of canned salmon and about 1⅓ cups (287 g) of the commercial food. If you increase it to 50 percent fresh food one or two days per week, that's okay. Your pet's nutrient balance won't be thrown off by one or two meals. You always have to keep the big picture in mind—what your meals look like for the week and for the entire month. Also, keep in mind that the more variety you have in your additions, the less you have to worry about percentages. If you're adding some canned salmon, some tahini, a spoonful of honey, and an egg, the balance starts working itself out perfectly. Another way to integrate the two diets is to feed a commercial diet four days a week and mix your own homemade meals three days a week.

One piece of advice: I would avoid adding too many carbohydrates as supplements to a commercial diet, because most commercial diets are already too high in carbs. But if you're using a high-protein/high-meat commercial diet, then adding ingredients such as carrots, barley, steamed broccoli, beet juice, oatmeal, etc., would be ideal. There are a lot of great new commercial diets out there, and many are specifically designed to allow you to add extras. (See Appendix 2 on page 170 for a listing of high-quality commercial food brands.)

Integrating Homemade Meals

When deciding to make homemade pet meals, be sure you take into account the time you have, your space, and the needs of other members of your household. These things will play a role in determining the kind of food you make and what ingredients you use. For example, grinding chicken necks in a meat grinder makes a mess, requires that the grinder be cleaned, and demands that you schedule time to defrost the necks. You can approach this issue by planning ahead or doing big batches at one time, or maybe you will have to decide against making recipes that include ground raw chicken necks. There are plenty of great meals to choose from, so don't feel that you have to use a specific recipe in order to give your pet optimum nutrition.

Observing Your Pet's Reaction

Consciously observing your pet and actively comparing different responses to various foods is probably the most important aspect of individualizing your homemade diet. The first six months to a year of a homemade diet is a particularly important time to be observant. But this awareness of your pet's well-being really is something that is lifelong. Most pets transition very easily to a homemade diet. But depending on your pet's eating background and age, he may need time to get accustomed to the new diet and get his health up to where it naturally should be.

I recommend that you start gradually, by adding one new ingredient to whatever your pet's regular meal has been, and do this for a couple of days. Note any reactions (good or bad) to the new addition. If you see negative reactions such as diarrhea, stop and go back to the old way of feeding for a few more days. Then try a different new food or a little less of the new food. Make note of anxiety and energy levels, too. If you see allergic reactions or dramatically negative reactions, stop adding new foods and go back to the original way of feeding until everything gets back to normal. This process may take a while, but it will be worth it!

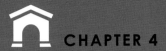

CHAPTER 4

Essential Building Blocks

Most of the homemade meals you make for your pet will consist of a meaty protein source, some fat, some bone or substitute calcium/mineral source, some greens and vegetables, and possibly some grain or seeds/nuts. Once you have a clear understanding of how these building blocks should be used and balanced, you'll be able to confidently individualize your pet's meals and provide a health-giving variety of ingredients.

Meats

Meat should be your main focus when making homemade pet food. About 60 to 75 percent of your pet's meals will be made up of meat of some sort, so this is where quality matters most. The meat will have fat in it and possibly bone. I don't want to focus on percentages, because you really need to keep it varied and individualized, but you do want a solid amount of protein in your cats' and dogs' diets.

Beef

Because cows are large animals, the texture of beef is coarse, and some cats and dogs really like it. Beef provides good chewing exercise and tooth-cleaning. Don't succumb to the low-fat craze here—you want to use beef with high levels of fat in it, but high-quality fat. Grass-fed beef is best, with omega-3 fatty acids naturally occurring in balanced form in the fat. If you are using non-grass-fed beef, then consider cutting the fat off the beef and substituting with a safer, more balanced fat such as that found in wild canned salmon, sardines, or butter from grass-fed cows.

I like to use chuck, round, or sirloin, which can be cut into appropriate-size chunks or ground up. These cuts are usually more than 15 percent fat. If you are using beef that is less than 15 percent fat, add 1/4 cup (56 g) of canned wild salmon, a couple of sardines, or a teaspoon of butter from grass-fed cows to each pound (455 g) of beef.

Good-quality, human-grade raw beef is perfectly safe to feed to cats and dogs; in fact, beef is harder for them to digest when it is cooked.

Lamb, Goat, and Venison

These meats provide great ways to add variety, even if cost and availability make them special-occasion meals. Beef and poultry are very common meat sources in commercial food, and many pets have developed sensitivities and allergies to them. In these cases, lamb, goat, and venison can be great alternative protein sources.

Poultry

Sizewise, poultry better matches what a cat or most dogs would hunt and kill in the wild. Be aware that there tends to be a higher ratio of antibiotics and hormones in poultry than in larger animals such as cows, so it is more important to find antibiotic-free, hormone-free, certified organic poultry. High-quality human-grade raw poultry is perfectly safe for cats and dogs to eat regularly. Raw, ground chicken necks are one of my favorite food ingredients to work with because they have a nice balance of bone in them. While cooked poultry tends to be very digestible for most pets, never feed your cat or dog cooked bones because they splinter easily.

Rabbit

I love the idea of feeding my pets rabbit meat, since wild cats and dogs use rabbit as a primary food source. The issue here is availability. Some people are lucky and have access to affordable rabbit meat. In other areas, rabbit meat is a gourmet delicacy and is expensive and hard to find. I am thrilled when one of my cats or dogs catches a wild rabbit, and I let them eat it as they please. The only issue I ever experienced with my pets eating wild rabbits is tapeworms. One of my cats contracted tapeworms, but only once. The deworming medication worked effectively, and I truly believe that the benefits of consuming a natural food source completely outweigh the potential problems from contracting worms.

Fish

The fish counter at the supermarket can be just as precarious to buy from as the meat aisle. Farm-raised fish usually have high levels of antibiotics and hormones. Farmed fish are fed unnatural diets, which makes their fat and meat unnaturally unbalanced. Smaller wild-caught fish are your best options. I like to buy the frozen whiting fillets, which are usually reasonably priced and conveniently fit into my meat grinder. I grind them while they are still frozen because it makes the job easier, then I let the food thaw thoroughly before serving. A word of warning: Do not feed raw salmon, farmed or wild, to dogs because they are susceptible to a serious parasitic infection from it.

Shellfish are full of nutrients, but I find that cats and dogs have very definite likes and dislikes in this category. So start with a small amount to test your animal's preferences before spending too much money on shellfish.

Canned wild Alaskan salmon is at the top on my list of super foods. I usually buy the type labeled as "pink" salmon, which is the least expensive. The salmon is cooked and includes a nice amount of tender and totally edible bones, providing a great calcium balance. Plus, salmon is high in animal-source omega-3 fatty acids.

Sardines are another great canned-fish option. I like the idea of canned fish because you can stock up and have it on hand. I buy the sardines with skins and bones for my animals, either packed in water or in olive oil. Like the canned salmon, they are wild caught and have a perfect balance of calcium and fats. Sardines are also small, so they are close to being whole foods and carry low mercury loads. They are also an ethical buying option because they are a very sustainable food source. In addition, canned jack mackerel and clams are good sources of taurine, as well as other essential nutrients.

You can alternate serving salmon, mackerel, and sardines. If you are serving salmon or mackerel, you will want to feed approximately the following minimum amounts:

- *Cat or small dog:* 1 tablespoon (10 g) daily

- *Medium dog:* 1 to 2 tablespoons (10 to 20 g) daily

- *Large dog:* ¼ cup (40 g) daily (about one-quarter of a can)

If you are serving sardines, you can feed the following amounts:

- *Cat or small dog:* ½ sardine daily

- *Medium dog:* 1 sardine daily

- *Large dog:* 2 or 3 sardines daily

I avoid fresh and canned tuna. Most is unethically harvested, and tuna's mercury and other pollutant levels are very high. Beyond that, cats have been known to get hooked on the flavor of tuna and then aren't drawn to eating other meats. It's best to just avoid it since there are so many better options.

Pork

Pork can be hard for your cat or dog to digest. A bite of cooked pork tenderloin or pork chop from the table would be fine, but don't feed raw pork—trichinosis is still a possible issue. And definitely avoid feeding any "preserved" or smoked pork products, such as ham, bacon, sausage, etc. They contain nitrates and nitrites. I wouldn't worry if you wanted to share some of the big batch of minestrone soup you made with pancetta or bacon in it; the goodness of the meal in general would be well worth the small exposure to the nitrates. Also, note there are now nitrate-free sources for these pork products that are well worth the extra expense.

Fats

In general, cats and dogs can get all the energy they need from fat and protein. But note that the fat they consume needs to be in balance with the amount of protein they are consuming, and the types of fat within the diet need to be in balance with one another. Essential Fatty Acids (EFAs) are the building blocks of fats that cannot be created within the body; it is therefore essential that we get them in the diet. Omega-3s and omega-6s are the two most important types that cats and dogs need.

Omega-3s

It is the quality of the fat that makes meat from a grass-fed animal so much better than the meat from a factory-raised animal. Omega-3s used to be common in our meat sources, but they are very delicate, subject to rancidity, and are not created in the flesh of animals eating an unnatural diet in crowded, dark production facilities. So in order to get beef with omega-3s, you have to find cows raised truly naturally—out in a field, eating pasture grass. And although omega-6 might be present in the beef of conventionally raised cows, it is out of balance, being without the omega-3, and I would have to suspect it's not as good as its counterpart in a grass-fed cow. This concept of the fat not being "right" in the meat from an unnaturally raised animal applies to all meat, from cows to chickens to fish.

Many pet nutritionists have addressed this problem by recommending lean meats and supplementing with oils such as flaxseed that are high in omega-3s. But flaxseed oil is a vegetable source and is not easily absorbed by carnivores. It is also extremely delicate and goes rancid very quickly. Dogs might be able to assimilate some omega-3s from plant sources, but they assimilate omega-3s better from meat sources. Cats cannot assimilate any omega-3 from vegetable sources and need to get all their EFAs from animal sources.

Try to get most of the fats you feed your pets from naturally raised animal meat. I realize this can be expensive, but I think it is necessary to go back to this natural way, support the farmers growing such meat, and accept the fact that you don't really want to be feeding your pet (or your human family!) cheap food.

Many cats and dogs show the typical outward signs of fatty acid deficiency: itchy, dry skin; excessive shedding; and dandruff. In fact, many people turn to creating a homemade pet diet because of these symptoms. But skin disorders are just the outward signs; the consumption of unbalanced, poor-quality, and rancid fats causes all sorts of damage to the health of cats and dogs, right down to the cellular and molecular level.

There Is an Easy Fix!

Beyond feeding your pet grass-fed and organic meat, you can boost the level of omega-3s in his or her meals by adding fish. Canned wild salmon, jack mackerel, and sardines all have high levels of quality omega-3s in the form of eicosapentaenoic acid (EPA) and docosahexaenoic acid (DHA), which are easily absorbed by cats and dogs. Using canned fish is so perfect. First, it is easy: You can stock up and always have it on hand. Second, it is an animal-based source. Third, it is a whole-food source of the fats, which is so much healthier than an oil that is processed and packaged, getting more and more rancid as it travels to a store and then to your house. See the Fish entry on page 47 for details on incorporating fish into your pet's diet.

There are also quite a few high-quality fish oil supplements available that are very effective at providing the extra omega-3s for balancing your pet's diet if you have trouble getting grass-fed meat. Choose a brand that is human-grade and encapsulated to ensure viability. Store in the refrigerator.

Because it is becoming clearer that pets need omega-3s in their diets, many pet food manufacturers are adding them to their foods. However, there is almost no way that the fragile omega-3s are actually still intact nutritionally by the time your pet eats the food. You would be much better off buying a food without the omega-3s added, and then adding a fresh source of omega-3s before serving.

Other, Not-So-Essential, Fats

Avocados are another good source for fats, particularly for dogs; cats can have a hard time digesting them. Despite anti-avocado myths, one avocado per week for a large dog would be very healthy. Cutting it up and feeding a couple of pieces throughout the week makes good sense.

Olive oil is another plant-based fat and good source of oleic acid, an omega-9 fatty acid. As with avocados, dogs assimilate olive oil better than cats do, but I have seen very good results in addressing dander issues in cats by adding $1/2$ teaspoon of olive oil to their meals. Use cold-pressed, extra-virgin olive oil. Cold pressing retains antioxidants and other nutrients. A teaspoon of oil per pound (455 g) of meat three times a week would be a healthy regular dosage.

Coconut oil is a saturated fat from plants, but the form of this fat is in medium-chain triglycerides, which are well-digested by pets and which help with the metabolism of fat-soluble vitamins. Use only virgin, unrefined coconut oil. It should be white when solid and clear when liquid. A maximum serving of 1 teaspoon (5 ml) per 10 pounds (4.5 kg) of body weight daily, split up into several servings, would be sufficient for integrating coconut oil into your pet's homemade diet.

One final note: Never feed your pet any hydrogenated oil such as margarine or partially hydrogenated soybean oil, or cottonseed oil.

Bones and Calcium

If your pet's diet is mostly based on whole foods, you will be able to balance the calcium fairly easily. For starters, feeding whole animal carcasses with bones would provide the optimal calcium balance. But when you are dealing with beef and other meat cuts and bone cuts that are available from grocery stores, you have to try to figure out how many bones would match the amount of meat you're feeding. And it is scary—we know never to feed cooked bones because they splinter very easily, but raw bones also splinter, cats and dogs do swallow bone fragments, and pets have been injured and killed by eating bones.

Yet many experts believe that bones are an essential element in the diet of cats and dogs, and that the risk is minimal and worth it. Others think that the safety risk demands other options.

Your pet absorbs calcium best when it is from animal sources and when other minerals are present in proper balance. Meat without bones is very high in phosphorus, and this phosphorus must be balanced with the proper amount of calcium. For cats, the ratio of calcium to phosphorus should be about 1:1; for dogs, plan for a little more calcium to phosphorus.

If you are using plain meat without bones, you can add bonemeal. Be sure to buy human-grade bonemeal that is free of heavy metals. Bonemeal is processed, but it is a whole food and contains a full range of minerals for proper calcium absorption. Use about 1 tablespoon (9 g) per 1 pound (455 g) of boneless meat.

Chicken Necks

These are a great source of calcium, and they not only have bone but also cartilage and meat. You can get chicken necks with the skin on, which provides fat. Keep in mind, though, that they do not have a lot of meat on them, so if you are feeding only the necks, you may end up serving your pet too much calcium. And if you are feeding only skin-on necks, you will be providing too much fat. To address this, I buy half my chicken necks without skin, and that balances the fat content nicely. I then make sure to add some other meat sources to my recipes with chicken necks, such as organ meats or fish. Chicken necks are very safe to feed whole, but most of my animals are not enthused with the idea of chewing on chicken necks, so I usually grind them up. It is easy to add other ingredients as I grind. Turkey necks would also work, but many home meat grinders will not be able to handle them.

Salmon

Canned wild pink Alaskan salmon is another very well-balanced ingredient to make use of. It contains meat as well as soft, edible bones and fat.

Carob

Although plant-based, carob powder has been used as a traditional supplemental calcium source for dogs in particular. Carob contains 28 milligrams of calcium in 1 tablespoon (9 g).

Eggshells

One eggshell has about 750 to 800 milligrams of calcium. If you use eggshell, you'll also be using the membranes on the inside of the shells that are full of nutrients. Eggshells can be sharp, though, and get more brittle with age. If you have your own chickens and can provide super-fresh eggshells, that would work nicely. But most grocery store eggs are already too old by the time they get on the shelves. So crush the egg-shells to a powder or run through your grinder, and they will be safe to add to your pet's food.

Kelp and Dulse

Kelp and dulse are see vegetables and are also a good calcium sources. The amount of calcium present in kelp can vary dramatically depending on the variety of kelp. Dried dulse can have more than 600 milligrams per ¼ cup (14 g).

Supplements

A calcium supplement is also an option. I prefer feeding my pets calcium lactate. One teaspoon per pound (455 g) of meat is usually sufficient.

As you can see, there are options beyond feeding bones to your pet, although bones are obviously the most natural choice. And not all bones splinter as readily as others. Inspect the bones you buy and use only thick, solid ones. My dogs love gnawing on big, raw beef shank bones. They get a look in their eyes when they are doing so that just seems primordial. I give them the shank bones more as a treat than as a calcium source. I have found that the bones from grass-fed cows are much stronger than the shank bones from conventionally raised cows.

Organ Meats

Organ meats are very important to include regularly in your home-made pet food. Of course, keep in mind that the organs make up a small percentage of the total food on a whole carcass, so don't overdo it. You want about one-sixth of your total diet plan to be made of organ meat, or about ¼ pound (115 g) of organ meat per week for a cat or small dog, ⅓ to ½ pound (151 to 225 g) for a medium dog, and ¾ to 1 pound (340 to 455 g) for a large dog. You can use mostly chicken and beef liver and hearts. Although the other organ meats are very good for your animals, they can be hard to find.

Liver

Because the liver is a cleansing organ, you should try to find certified organic liver. You will see a huge difference in color between an organic liver, which is a dark, velvety purple-brown, and a non-organic one, which is a tan-red color with mushy consistency.

Hearts

Beef and chicken hearts must be added into your pet's diet. Hearts are the main sources of the amino acids most needed by cats and dogs, including taurine and carnitine. Eggs and raw, dark meat chicken also contain some taurine, but I recommend a taurine or amino acid complex supplement or a multivitamin containing taurine for your pet if you aren't able to feed raw hearts regularly.

Eggs

Pasture-raised, organic-sourced eggs are super foods. Do not split up yolk from white. The nutrients of the yolk and white work together and are in a good nutritional ratio with one another. Large amounts of raw egg white fed on a regular basis have been linked to biotin deficiencies, so be sure to always use the whole egg and don't feed eggs every single day. I usually use eggs every other day in my meal plans.

Eggs are awesome sources of the full range of vitamins and minerals and contain all the essential amino acids as well as perfect fats. Remember, a whole new life has all it needs to come to fruition in an egg.

Raw whole eggs can be added easily to ground meat recipes, making the consistency more appealing. I use about one egg per pound (455 g) of meat.

Cooked eggs work fine in most cases too, although they can be a bit harder for your pet to digest the more cooked they are. I avoid hard-cooking for the most part and instead serve my pet eggs that are sunny-side up or lightly scrambled. I also love to make frittatas of various sorts for my animals.

Be aware that there are huge differences in nutrient levels, including levels of omega-3 fatty acids, between organic, pasture-raised eggs and conventional eggs. Truly naturally raised eggs are nutritionally complete.

Seeds: Legumes, Nuts, and Grains

Like eggs, seeds are wonderful super foods. Legumes (beans), nuts, and grains are all seeds. Some are more easily digested by cats and dogs than others. I hardly ever use beans intentionally in my animals' meals, though they do get some because beans are a big part of the human meals I make and share with my pets.

Nuts

I often add nuts to my pets' meals because nuts have a wonderful array of healthy fats when raw and fresh. Dogs are better able than cats to make use of the fats and other nutrients in nuts. I avoid buying nut oils because they are always expensive and tend to go rancid very fast. I buy nuts in bulk and freeze them to keep them as fresh as possible. Dogs and cats don't have the ability within their digestive systems to break down whole nuts effectively. They usually pass right through, so I grind most of the nuts with my meat grinder as I grind the meat. The best nuts to use are walnuts, almonds, pecans, pignoli (pine nuts), and Brazil. I avoid macadamia nuts because they have had certain toxicities associated with them. I also avoid peanuts, which can have high levels of mold that can produce aflatoxin.

Three Wonderful Seeds

I like to use **sesame seeds** in my dog and cat food. Despite their small size, they need to be ground. Buy either hulled or unhulled sesame seeds that look bright and golden in color; avoid grayish dull ones, which indicate age. You can also use tahini, a paste made from sesame seeds. I try to find tahini that is made from unroasted sesame seeds, as opposed to roasted.

Sunflower seeds are another favorite of mine. I regularly grind them into my pet food recipes. Again, be sure to find fresh, raw seeds. They are full of B vitamins as well as other life-supporting vital nutrients.

Pumpkin seeds (hulled; also called pepitas) are also very nutritious for pets. Like all seeds and nuts, pumpkin seeds have tons of nutrients packed inside them, especially magnesium, phosphorus, potassium, and zinc. In addition, they are highly effective at removing intestinal worms quickly and gently, due to a rare amino acid referred to as cucurbitin. Just six to twelve (depending on the size of the animal) pumpkin seeds ground and mixed into each meal daily for a period of seven days is usually a very effective deworming protocol. In tougher cases, feeding for fourteen days should be sufficient. Pumpkin seeds also contain a protein called myosin that plays an important role in the chemistry of healthy muscles. They are truly super foods!

Grains

Cats and dogs have no real nutritional need for grains in their diets. Pet food manufacturers use grain because it is a cheap source of filler and adds protein and calories to the label on the bag. But these are empty numbers for most cats and dogs because they don't absorb nutrients from grains in the same way we do. In fact, many animals have developed sensitivities or allergies to certain grains. Corn and soy also tend to have genetically modified organisms (GMOs) and should be avoided unless certified organic or certified GMO–free.

Having said that, grains can be used in the diets of cats and dogs in moderation. Grains have many minerals and vitamins and can be a cost-effective way to bulk up your food and stick to a budget. This is not a bad thing—your pet will surely benefit from the food when you make it yourself whether you use grains or not, and you have to make this work for you. I have found that many large-breed dogs actually do better and keep a better weight when their diet includes high-quality grains. I often cook beets in water for my household, and when I look at the leftover dark, antioxidant-rich purple beet water that remains, I am very happy to pour some rolled oats in and let them cook and soak up the nutrients to feed to my animals. You can make vegetable-enriched grains out of any leftover veggie cooking liquid; just add enough water to cook the grains fully. I then usually add a spoonful of these veggie oats to my ground-meat meals for a little variation and to make the food last longer.

Keep in mind that grains must all be cooked well. I prefer to use oats, barley, millet, and brown rices in pet food. Corn/polenta is usually well-liked, but it can disagree with some pets or instigate allergies. Cats will need their grains mixed well with meat—use about four parts meat to one part grain in cat food. For dogs, aim for about two parts meat to one part grain. Don't get overly hung up on these ratios; variety is good, and you will have to adjust according to your individual animal's needs.

Vegetables and Fruits

Vegetables look like the epitome of good health, so we tend to pile them into our pet's food. That's actually not so bad because the antioxidants in vegetables and fruits will protect against cancer and support health in so many ways. Aim for about ¼ cup (30 g) of minced or mashed vegetables per pound (455 g) of meat, or ⅓ cup (40 g) minced or mashed vegetables for each cup of grain and 2 cups (450 g) meat. You should use more vegetables than fruits. I usually pick the more colorful ones, but again, your aim is to provide variety.

The key to proper feeding of vegetables is to keep rotating and mixing them up. And remember that you are actually doing the opposite ratio for your pets than you would do for humans. The human body requires mostly vegetables and some meats; our pets should be eating mostly meats and some vegetables.

To make sure your cat or dog can absorb the nutrients in vegetables, finely mince or gently cook them. Some vegetables lend themselves better than others to this treatment. Vegetables that are great to serve cooked as well as raw are asparagus, celery, cabbage, beets, broccoli, cauliflower, corn, turnips, and summer squash. Vegetables that really should be cooked for better digestion in cats and dogs are sweet potatoes (baked), winter squash (steamed or baked), peas, and green beans.

I mince vegetables in a food processor or by running them through my meat grinder as I am grinding meat. I cook most vegetables by cutting them into chunks and steaming. You can also just cook up the vegetables as you would for yourself, such as sautéing them in olive oil with some garlic and spices, and then share them with your animals. I've found that cats tend to prefer cooked and mashed vegetables over raw and minced ones.

Vegetables and fruits that I usually feed only raw and minced are cucumbers, berries, greens, sprouts, apples, and watermelons.

Don't overlook the unappealing (to humans) parts of vegetables and fruits. Make use of broccoli and cauliflower stalks, carrot skins, watermelon rinds, fennel fronds, and so forth. They contain all the nutrients the rest of the plant has. Simply grind them up and add them to your pet's food.

Carrots are a particular favorite of my animals; they work well raw and ground up as well as cooked in all different ways. I wash them and cut the top shoulders off, but I leave the skins on. I am happy to note that my dogs' teeth get cleaned when I give them whole raw carrots to munch on. Baby carrots and carrot sticks can also be healthy alternatives to dog biscuits, especially for grain-sensitive dogs.

There are some canned vegetables that work fine in a pinch. Canned carrots, green beans, corn, peas, and pumpkin certainly can be employed as time-saving ways to incorporate easily digestible vegetables and fruit into your pet's diet.

Avoid vegetables in the nightshade family such as tomatoes, peppers, eggplants, and potatoes. I would be especially aware of elderly pets' reactions to these vegetables, as they can aggravate arthritis. Although I don't specifically plan pet meals with nightshades, if I'm sharing a spaghetti dinner with my pets, I don't fret over the tomato sauce, which has nutritional benefits, such as lycopene, and is quite digestible when well cooked.

Cats are very individualistic when it comes to vegetables. Steamed broccoli and cooked peas tend to be favorites with my cats. Some cats go crazy over raw cucumbers and asparagus. Nothing is funnier than a cat darting out of the asparagus patch with an asparagus spear in her mouth!

Dark, Leafy Greens

Although calcium from dark, leafy greens is readily absorbed by humans, carnivores such as cats and dogs can't really make good use of this form of calcium, and many dark greens are high in oxalic acid, which can interfere with calcium absorption if too much is fed regularly. However, dark, leafy greens are nutrient-rich, power-packed foods, and dogs and cats both have a tendency to seek them out and munch on them in the yard.

For this reason, I put dark, leafy greens in a category by themselves, separate from vegetables, because I think of them as more of a super-food supplement. One to 2 teaspoons is good for a cat or small dog, 3 to 4 tablespoons (6 to 8 g) for a medium dog, and up to $1/3$ cup (10 g) for a large dog, fed every other day or so. This is not only perfectly safe but also tremendously health giving. Be sure to finely mince dark, leafy greens or pass them through the food processor or your meat grinder.

Incorporate all types of dark, leafy greens—spinach, kale, collards, broccoli raab, lettuces, chard, cabbage, and chicories—into your pet's diet. Arugula is a big favorite of many dogs; one of our farm CSA members is a Saint Bernard who sniffs out the arugula in her share basket on her trip home. And make use of parsley regularly; it is jam-packed with minerals and phytonutrients. You can use fresh parsley or dried. You can also include mild herbs in your dark, leafy greens portion. I've used sorrel, dill, mint, basil, fennel, oregano, and cilantro. Many cats really enjoy herbs; one of my cats adores borage leaves. Take a look around your yard for chickweed, plantain, dandelion, purslane, and other edible wild greens to add to your pet's diet.

Fiber or Roughage

You need to incorporate fiber into your pet's diet to make up for the fur and other rough, fibrous particles that would inevitably be swallowed by a wild cat or dog while dining on a carcass. Some experts recommend a bit of wheat bran, and others recommend psyllium husk powder. You want to be careful that you provide enough water with these ingredients. I use them occasionally, but I also believe that the ground nuts and minced vegetables in my recipes will provide my pets with adequate roughage. Grains also do the job. If you were feeding a pure meat meal, you might consider sprinkling about 1 teaspoon of wheat bran over about 1 pound (455 g) of meat, especially if you notice your pet is having difficulty passing stool, or passes very hard stools.

Dairy

There is much contention among animal nutritionists about feeding dairy to cats and dogs. Obviously, full-grown cats and dogs in the wild don't have access to dairy products. However, dairy products have been fed to cats and dogs for a long time without harm. I find that they can be very useful in the diet, but you may decide to avoid them, depending on your individual animal's reaction.

Start with simpler meals made with dairy to get a clear idea of how your pet reacts. Watch for diarrhea, gas, and gurgling stomach noises. Cats with Siamese genetic backgrounds (a thin, angular head shape would be a possible indicator of this genetic history) seem to have a particular sensitivity to dairy.

Cheese and Butter

Avoid hard cheeses in chunks. A little is fine as a treat or shaved or grated over food. But I have found that many dogs who swallow whole chunks of hard cheese have a tendency to vomit them back up pretty much undigested. Cheddar cheese has a tooth-cleansing property that is great to take advantage of if your dog or cat adequately chews the cheese pieces. I give a slice of Cheddar as a treat in a calm situation where I know my animals will take the time to chew it, enabling the cheese to lessen buildup on their teeth quite effectively. Soft cheeses such as cottage cheese, farmer's cheese, and goat cheese all can be great additions to your pet's diet. I like to smear a soft white cheese over a piece of sprouted-grain bread as a quick breakfast for myself and my animals.

If you'd like to offer your cat or dog butter, just a couple pats of butter from grass-fed cows added to their food can help in balancing fats.

As with all foods, you want to find the most natural sources of dairy products. Always purchase dairy products that are free of rBGH (recombinant bovine growth hormone). Try to get organic, which would be antibiotic free, and try to get grass-fed. Grass-fed dairy will include the omega-3 oils that are so important to get into your pet's diet (see "Omega-3s" on page 50). You want the dairy products you use to be as alive and unprocessed as possible. If you can find dairy products that haven't been homogenized or pasteurized, so much the better. Unpasteurized or raw milk is available now in many states.

Yogurt

Yogurt is another great ingredient you can incorporate into your pet's diet. Buy yogurt in as natural a form as possible, with natural cultures and enzymes. These will provide important beneficial bacteria (probiotics) your pets need for a healthy digestive system. Avoid yogurt with sweeteners or flavorings added.

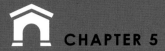

CHAPTER 5

Fine-Tuning Your Homemade Meal Plan

In the previous chapter, we discussed the essential building blocks (main ingredient categories) that you'll be basing your homemade pet meals on: meats, fats, bones and calcium, organ meats, eggs, seeds, vegetables and fruits, leafy greens, fiber, and dairy. Beyond what we discussed in chapter 4, there are other fresh, whole foods to be considered as you fine-tune your pet's meal plan.

Species-Appropriate Super Foods

The following "super foods" can add a variety of nutrients to your pet's diet and address possible nutrient deficiencies as well.

Alfalfa

Some super foods contain a gamut of important nutrients, and alfalfa is one of those. I keep a jar of alfalfa powder on hand and sprinkle some into my pets' meals for an extra boost of nutrients. Alfalfa sprouts are also a great addition. One of my cats adores alfalfa and mung bean sprouts; I drop a few on the floor, and she bats them around before gobbling them down.

Aniseed and Fennel Seed

I first read about aniseed and fennel seed in Juliette de Baïracli Levy's classic and inspiring books on natural animal care. Since then, these two seed powders have held an important place in my pet food cabinet. Although they are providing many of the same nutrients and minerals as the other ingredients mentioned in this chapter, these seeds are providing these nutrients in a new form and in different ratios—a perfect way to incorporate variety. Fennel is also a great vegetable to add to your pet food mixes.

Garlic

Although in the onion family, garlic is safe when used in moderation. Do not overdo it, because in large amounts garlic has the potential to act like onions and cause Heinz body anemia in cats. If your pet has exhibited sensitivities or has a preexisting anemic condition, do not feed garlic. Also, avoid feeding garlic to animals younger than six months old.

Garlic is, however, a very healthy addition to a pet's diet; it is an antioxidant, antibacterial, antiviral, immune system stimulant and general health tonic. I try to vary the way I use garlic because its phytochemicals differ when the garlic is fresh than when it is exposed to oxygen for varying amounts of time, and when it is cooked and/or dried.

Dogs usually really love garlic, but you may find that cats are not as into garlic as dogs, and some cats may get turned off from trying new foods if they smell garlic. Let them guide you—if they really don't want to eat food with garlic, then just skip it. You're already adding plenty of other super-healthy ingredients into your cat's diet. My rule of thumb for serving garlic is to add about 1/8 teaspoon of powdered garlic per pound (455 g) of meat, or one clove of fresh garlic for 5 to 7 pounds (2275 to 3185 g) of meat.

Honey

Another super food to definitely keep in your cabinet, honey has amazing healing powers. Although I am not an advocate of adding sweeteners to pet food, honey is an important exception. Honey has so many life-giving benefits, and the sweetness of a dollop of honey added to the food can make a finicky pet—or a pet who has gotten used to sugary commercial food—better enjoy the meal.

Kelp and Dulse

These seaweeds contain a marvelous plethora of nutrients, and particularly minerals. I eat kelp myself, I feed it to my chickens, I use it in my garden, and, of course, I include it in my pet food. There are many different species of kelp, but the three most common for human consumption are kombu, arame, and wakame, and these are what I feed my animals.

Dulse is a red species of seaweed that contains different nutrients than kelp. I like combining the two seaweeds in a 1:1 ratio, although if you only use kelp, that is fine too. Seaweed is high in iodine, so don't feed more than ½ teaspoon to a cat or small dog, 1 teaspoon to a medium dog, or 2 teaspoons to a large dog per day.

Parsley

Parsley is so much more than a garnish—it is another super food, full of minerals and chlorophyll. Parsley emanates life and restores well-being and vitality right down to the cellular level. I add minced fresh parsley whenever I can to my pets' (and my) meals, and use dried when I don't have fresh available. It also makes the meal look very pretty! I sometimes add dried parsley to hot water and brew a tea. After it cools, I pour it into my animals' water bowls to give them an extra nutrient boost.

Turmeric

Although most spices provide wonderful variety and a solid array of nutrients, I focus mainly on turmeric for pet food recipes. Turmeric is a powerful antioxidant and anti-inflammatory, and is worthy of being included in many pet meals each week. It doesn't have a strong flavor, and the antioxidants in it will turn the food a delightful yellow color.

Herb and Spice Healthy Supplement Powder

Make a big batch of this powder. Once pre-mixed, it is easy to add a bit to your pet's meals each day or so.

1 cup (160 g) kelp powder
1 cup (56 g) dulse flakes
1 cup (112 g) turmeric powder
1 cup (70 g) alfalfa powder
1 cup (21 g) dried parsley or **nettle**
½ cup (24 g) dried oregano
¼ cup (24 g) aniseed or **fennel powder**
⅛ cup (13 g) garlic powder (less for cats)

In a large bowl, combine all ingredients and mix thoroughly. Pour into a glass jar and store tightly covered in a cool, dry place. Mix the following amounts into your pet's meal: ¼ teaspoon per day for a cat or small dog, ½ teaspoon for a medium dog, or 1 teaspoon for a large dog.

Antioxidants: A Rainbow of Colors

These colors represent various phytochemicals that can help fight cancer, increase brain function, rejuvenate cells, and so much more! Pick and choose a variety that reflects what you have available seasonally, locally, or on sale at the grocery store and add them to your pet's diet.

Color	Food Sources	Health Benefits
Red	Apples, beets, radishes, raspberries, red pears, strawberries, watermelon	The nutrients in red and red-skinned vegetables and fruits help maintain a strong heart and brain, lower risk of certain cancers, and strengthen urinary tract function. These are also good sources for vitamin C.
Orange and yellow	Carrots, corn, melons, pineapple, sweet potatoes, winter squash, yellow apples, yellow beets, yellow summer squash	Yellow pigments provide antioxidants that are beneficial to the eyes as well as the heart and immune system. They are also noted for their ability to lower risk of certain cancers. High in vitamin C and folate.
White and brown	Bananas, cabbage, cauliflower, garlic, parsnips, pears, summer squash, turnips	Although lacking in strong color-related antioxidants, these fruits and vegetables make up for it with strong flavor-related phytonutrients, which provide DNA and heart disease protection, and boost the immune system. They also contain some of the strongest proven cancer-fighting phytonutrients.
Green	Arugula, asparagus, avocados, broccoli, celery, chard, collards, cress, green apples, green beans, honeydew melons, kales, lettuce, parsley, peas, spinach	Green foods, and particularly the cruciferous vegetables, lower the risk of certain cancers. These chlorophyll-related antioxidants also are known to reduce heart disease, maintain healthy eyes, protect against birth defects, and keep red blood cells healthy.
Blue, violet, and black	Bilberries, blackberries, blueberries, mulberries, red cabbage	The deep blue pigments have some of the highest antioxidant activity. These strengthen brain function, protect against certain cancers, improve urinary tract function, promote heart health, and more.

Essential Nutrients

By providing your pet with all of these wonderful whole foods in their daily meals, you should have no issues with providing all the essential nutrients your pet needs to thrive. There is a selection of nutrients that are available in supplement form and that are considered very important that I will discuss in brief at right. Always follow the directions for dosages on the supplement packaging you are using and/or consult a veterinarian.

Vitamin A

Vitamin A is naturally present in perfect, bioavailable form in raw meat, fish, and eggs. Alfalfa, kelp, and vegetables add even more vitamin A in varied forms. I don't recommend using cod-liver oil unless you are addressing a vitamin A deficiency. With a varied fresh diet, your pet is almost certainly getting enough vitamin A.

The B Vitamins (B-Complex)

The B vitamins are present in varying degrees in meats (especially grass-fed, organic meat), fish, whole grains, and eggs. Vegetables, nuts, seeds, alfalfa, and kelp add more. So if you are providing a varied diet of whole fresh foods, your levels of the B vitamins should be optimal. You might consider a B-complex supplement if your pet is going through a stressful period; if so, use a B-complex made for pets and follow the directions on the supplement packaging or consult your veterinarian.

Vitamin C

Although vitamin C is present in vegetables, fruit, alfalfa, and kelp, as well as meat, I usually add an extra 500 to1000 milligrams of buffered C or ester C in my weekly batches of pet food. Vitamin C is a nutrient that can become depleted very quickly when an animal is under stress.

Vitamin D

Animals get vitamin D from exposure to sunlight as well as from the eggs and meat of pasture-raised or grass-fed animals. If you are not feeding pasture-raised or grass-fed meat, consider a vitamin D_3 supplement for your pet; follow the directions for dosage on the supplement package or consult your veterinarian.

Vitamin E

A very important nutrient, vitamin E is present in quality eggs, as well as in fish, meat, nuts and seeds, alfalfa, and kelp.

Minerals and Trace Minerals

For calcium to be easily absorbed, the other minerals must all be present and in proper balance. That is why it is so important to feed whole food ingredients and choose foods that are pecies-appropriate. Beyond meat and bone, herbs, nuts, seeds, dairy, grains, and dark, leafy greens provide a variety of mineral sources.

Amino Acids

Cats and dogs have slightly different needs for amino acids than we humans do. Raw organ meats (particularly hearts) combined with muscle meat will provide pets with a solid balance of amino acids. However, if you do not feed raw organ meats, do include a high-quality amino acid complex made specifically for cats or dogs; follow the directions for dosage on the supplement package or consult your veterinarian.

Probiotics and Digestive Enzymes

Yogurt is a whole food option for providing your cat or dog with probiotics, but many people prefer not to feed their pets dairy. And most pets could benefit from a boost of both digestive enzymes and probiotics. Choose a quality pet-enzyme formula. I prefer one that is made of whole food ingredients rather than just synthetic nutrients.

Multivitamin Supplement

It's wise to purchase a high-quality species-specific multivitamin to have on hand for days when you do simpler meals and want to add an extra boost of vitamins.

There are probably thousands of other nutrients beyond the well-researched ones I've included in this chapter, but that's the beauty of feeding your pet a diet made up of whole, fresh foods—by providing variation and high-quality meals, you will have all your bases covered.

You may be wondering why, if a cat or dog could live very healthfully on a diet of just mice and rabbits, do we need all these extras?

First of all, we're not feeding our cats and dogs whole, wild mice and rabbits. The meat we are feeding our pets is actually too clean—there is no fur or feathers, no dirt. And beyond the hearts and livers, we are missing the other organs like the brain, stomach, intestines, contents of viscera, etc. Also, if your pet has been eating only commercial food, he or she may need a boost to get back to optimal health. Current conventional pet food production has sacrificed nutrients for high productivity and higher monetary returns. Unless we are buying organic and sustainably produced vegetables and grains and pastured eggs, dairy, and meats, we are feeding our pets foods with reduced amounts of nutrients, and we need to find ways to make up for this loss.

Beyond all this, I think pets today are dealing with more environmental stresses than ever before. Modern household life, with its array of electronics and flashing high-definition screens, combined with chemical onslaughts and human household members with busier and busier lives, takes a toll on our pets. It is our responsibility to address this by providing support through optimum nutrition in their meals.

Foods to Avoid

I wholeheartedly encourage you to be creative with ingredients and provide your animals with lots of variety. However, there are some foods that you need to avoid putting in your pet food.

Chocolate

If your large dog accidentally eats a chocolate chip, it is nothing to panic over, but large quantities can be harmful. Avoid allowing your animals access to chocolate, especially dark chocolate.

Extra Omega-6 Oils

I can assure you that you probably have enough omega-6 oils in your pet food. Focus on providing high-quality, non-rancid, animal-source omega-3 oils instead. Or for variation in oils, use some olive oil or coconut oil.

Hydrogenated Fats

Never feed margarine or any partially hydrogenated fats to your pets. These are unnatural forms of fat that wreak havoc on the body.

Lecithin

Almost all lecithin is made from soy, and almost all soy has genetically modified organisms (GMOs). You can now find non-soy, non-GMO lecithin in stores, but it is not species-appropriate, and you can easily provide your pet with plenty of nutrients from the other species-appropriate ingredients we have been discussing.

Onions

This category includes onions as well as other members of the allium family, such as leeks, shallots, chives, and scallions. They can cause a life-threatening disorder, called Heinz body anemia. Don't create meals for your pets and purposely add onions of any sort.

Raisins and Grapes

Do not feed these to your pets, ever. They have been linked to urinary dysfunction and even kidney failure.

Yeast

Although many pet nutritionists and supplement companies recommend use of yeast, I do not use it. Most yeast products for pets are of substandard industry waste-product quality. But even high-quality nutritional yeast is not species-appropriate—it is a fungal product and one that can easily promote various pet health issues, particularly skin conditions. I believe that many hot spot and other skin disorders are caused by yeast overgrowth in the body, aggravated by the consumption of supplementary yeast. Overgrowth of yeast is known to instigate digestive and urinary tract issues as well. Yeast also has high levels of phosphorus, which can unbalance the calcium ratio in your meals.

Top Ten Herbs for Pets

There are tons of herbs that address health issues and problems, but these ten are especially potent at providing necessary nutrients for general health and well-being.

- Aniseed (*Pimpinella anisum*)

- Borage (*Borago officinalis*)

- Catnip/catmint (*Nepeta cataria*)

- Chickweed (*Stellaria media*)

- Dill (*Anethum graveolens*)

- Fennel and fennel seed (*Foeniculum vulgare*)

- Oat grass, also known as catgrass (*Avena sativa*)

- Oregano (*Origanum vulgare*)

- Parsley (*Petroselinum crispum*)

- Stinging nettle (*Urtica dioica*)

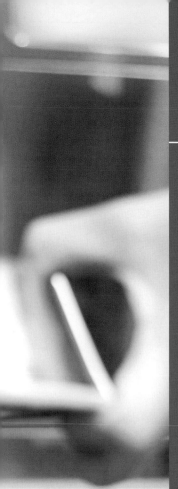

CHAPTER 6

Switching to a Homemade Diet

You will need only an operational kitchen to make your own pet food—nothing beyond what you use to regularly prepare human food.

Kitchen Readiness

The one piece of equipment you'll need to prepare homemade pet food that you might not have already is a meat grinder. Grinders come in different sizes. I use my small household grinder almost every week, and it allows me to grind chicken necks as well as other meats and vegetables all together at one time. A larger grinder would provide more flexibility, allowing you to grind ingredients such as chicken legs, turkey necks, and even larger bones.

A food processer would also be very useful because you will be grinding nuts and seeds and mincing herbs and greens regularly. A high-quality food processor is well worth the extra money since it will make mincing and grinding even small amounts of ingredients fast and efficient. I also like to use a mezzaluna to hand-chop and mince. Although it takes more time, I feel like I am more a part of my food making, adding intentions and good positive thoughts, which I find difficult to do when there is a loud motor doing the chopping for me. It's also good to have storage containers on hand that you've reserved for pet food use only.

What follows are some specific techniques you'll be using as you prepare your pet's meals, along with suggestions for serving and storing foods.

Freezing

It is usually easier to grind meat pieces when they are cold or partially frozen. Grinders create heat during use, and the fats in the meat can glob up the machine's pieces and cause clogs. But when meat is ground very cold, the consistency of the ground meat is chunkier and firmer, rather than pasty, and tends not to clog. Whenever I grind meats, I alternate during the process between meat and vegetables so the vegetables can help clear out the fat buildup in the grinder and keep the food processing nicely.

Although freezing degrades the nutritional quality of meat to some extent, the amount of degradation surely doesn't compete with the convenience of it. Many pet food nutritionists are against feeding any meat that was frozen, but I find it very hard to schedule the purchase of fresh meat on a day-to-day basis. I freeze almost all my meat because I buy it in bulk and it grinds better when it is at least slightly frozen. I then refreeze much of it in serving-size portions after I grind and mix in the other ingredients.

Plating It Up: Serving Suggestions

When feeding cooked food, let it cool down to room temperature before serving. With raw food or with food you made in large batches and stored in the refrigerator, leave the food out on the counter to warm up. You can also place the food in a bowl of hot water to speed up the process, but don't microwave it. Microwaving destroys and changes the nutrients you worked so hard to include. I recommend feeding all foods at room temperature because a wild cat or dog would be eating their meat either warm with life or at least at room temperature most of the time, never ice cold.

Avoid using plastic pet food bowls. I usually use ceramic bowls from my own dining set—they then get put in the dishwasher each night with the rest of the dishes. Metal bowls are fine to use too; just make sure you keep them clean. When you feed raw meat-based meals or even cooked meals, the food residue left in the bowls is much more likely to rot and putrefy than when feeding dry kibble.

Mealtime

The digestive systems of cats and (to a slightly lesser extent) dogs are dependent on certain clues to fully start up and get ready for digestion. For this reason, allowing your pet to exercise before eating is very beneficial because it mimics the carnivore chasing down its prey. Exercise after eating is not healthy. Your pet's after-eating environment should be calm and peaceful as digestion occurs.

The smell of food is also an important prerequisite to eating. Keep this in mind as you prepare the food; your pet is smelling the food and watching you get it ready—this is healthy. When a cat or dog anticipates a meal, certain changes happen within the digestive system; blood flow to the stomach increases and decreases throughout the rest of the body. When the meal is ready to be served, your pet's metabolism is ready to use the very most of all the nutrients in it.

Keeping this in mind, don't free-feed or leave food available all day long. This is fine with herbivores, but with carnivores, it can be detrimental. You don't want your pet to be in a constant state of digestive alertness; this would eventually weaken his or her entire system. Free-feeding has also been associated with feline urologic syndrome. So only leave food out for about 20 minutes to a half hour. If not all of it is eaten within that time, take the remainder back and put it away in the fridge or throw it away.

The time of day to feed is up to you; make it whenever it is convenient. Despite what many pet owners believe, your pet doesn't need to eat at the same time every day. I usually feed my cats and dogs twice a day—a light breakfast and a heavier dinner. Kittens and puppies, and some individual animals, will need more feedings per day, while some cats and dogs will do best when fed once per day.

Keeping It Safe and Clean

Although raw meat is safe for your carnivore pet to consume, keep aware that you, and especially the human children in your household, should not consume raw meat. Don't let children touch the used, uncleaned pet food bowls without washing their hands afterward. Pick up the used bowls and wash them as soon as possible. Thoroughly wash down all kitchen surfaces that you prepared the pet food on. And be sure to wash your own hands after all food prep!

Storing Your Pet's Meals

Treat your pet's food as you would your own. When storing pet food, keep it cold and in airtight containers. I prefer glass to plastic storage containers, but you do have a lot more options in sizes in plastic. Plastic is also lighter for easier cleaning. But plastic ages badly; once you see scratches and discoloration, discard plastic containers. Also, don't let aluminum foil come in contact with the food. I usually cover the food with a sheet of waxed paper, and then use aluminum foil or plastic wrap over that to seal.

Also, if you are using canned fish or vegetables in your pet meal recipes and don't use a whole can at once, dump the extra into a bowl or other container for storage. Don't leave food in the fridge in an opened can. Oxidation starts up fast and strong once air gets to the interior of the metal can, and so it is best not to leave food in contact with it at that point.

Making the Switch

As I've said throughout this book, take your time with introducing your pet to his or her new home-made diet. Start by adding fresh foods that you know your pet likes to the commercial pet food you have been feeding. If you are already making your own food, try adding a couple new ingredients each week. Keep the new food introductions simple.

This gradual approach is especially important with some cats, who may not only be finicky about trying new foods, but can also get turned off from all new foods because of one particularly offensive experience. One thing I usually suggest to cat owners is to allow the cat onto the kitchen table during meals and let the cat take a look and smell the different foods. You don't need to let the cat eat off your plate, but you can give small mouth-fuls of different types of food to the cat to try. The pressure is off this way—the cat thinks he is just checking out your food, not being forced to eat something he doesn't like. It also gives you an idea of what your cat likes and passes up, and presents it all in a low-stress manner.

Some pets will take to the new diet with perfect ease. Others may find the transition a bit stressful, wanting the routine of the commercial food. Many commercial pet food brands contain ingredients that have almost addictive effects on cats and dogs, so you may find switching away from those brands more difficult. It is worth the effort, though, so keep at it.

Some pets may experience some digestive upset as their systems adjust to the new food, especially if they have been eating the exact same food every single day their whole lives. Many commercial foods have stool-stabilizing ingredients in them that help the pet form a normal-looking stool. Animals who eat this type of food can become dependent on the stool stabilizer and have very loose stools once they are off that food. Be patient; your animal's system will get used to the new food and be able to digest and thrive on it eventually.

If your pet has diarrhea or gassiness, cut back on the new food. You can do this by simply going back to the old food, or by taking away a couple of the new ingredients and simplifying the new food additions. Consider putting your pet on a one-day fast to help clear out his or her system and detoxify. Watch your pet and note the reactions to the new food. If you suspect any particular ingredient is instigating a bad reaction or causing an allergic reaction, stop feeding that ingredient. Be observant and patient. You may be very excited to switch your pet over to this fabulous new food, but your pet may need time to adjust.

One more note on stool: When you are transitioning from a commercial diet of mostly cooked and dry food to a homemade one of raw and fresh foods, you'll notice your pet's stool will be much smaller and darker. This is because the fresh food is highly digestible. Owners are sometimes alarmed by how little stool is produced, thinking something is wrong. But this is a good thing because it is proof that your pet is digesting more of the food, and the bonus is that there is less poop to clean up!

CHAPTER 7

Healthy Homemade Recipes

You'll be feeding your pet an amazing, health-giving diet by building each meal starting with meat and fat. You also need to make sure you have an adequate calcium source for balancing the amount of meat. And be sure you have organ meats and other extras such as nuts; vegetables; dark, leafy greens; and/or other whole, fresh food supplements containing the extra essentials nutrients.

Following in this chapter is a selection of some of my favorite recipes, which I hope will inspire you. Don't feel compelled to follow these recipes exactly item by item. Feel free to be creative and make substitutions with ingredients that are available and that match your individual pet's needs and preferences. Keep the essential pet food building blocks in mind as your basic guidelines, and plan on providing a variety of food types over the course of the week. Your pet's homemade diet will be awesome!

Getting Started

Some recipes yield a single serving or just a couple of servings, while others are large enough to feed a large dog for three or four days. I developed these recipes according to how I usually prepare meals; some ingredients such as chicken necks are best used in bulk because the cleanup is messy and you might as well make a lot if you are going to have to spend the time cleaning up the grinder and kitchen. Other ingredients, such as sardines, come in small, neat packages and are easy to use on a day-to-day basis.

Many of these recipes are easy to make in large amounts, which usually saves you cost and time, even if you are not a multiple-animal household. Feel free to double or triple these recipes. They will keep just fine for several days in the refrigerator, and most can be frozen as well.

For the recipes using chicken necks, I usually start with 40 pounds (18 kg) of chicken necks, which is typically the price break for bulk. Forty pounds of necks is also usually how much my grinder can grind before it needs to be cleaned out if I use partially frozen necks and am careful to alternate vegetables for every ten or so necks.

I end up with a huge batch of food once the other ingredients are added. At that point, I roll the mixture into serving-size meatballs for each size cat or dog. I place them on a baking sheet in a single layer and freeze them. Once frozen, I put the meatballs into freezer bags for efficient storing. Then I just take out whatever number of meatballs is needed for the next couple of days and defrost them in the refrigerator. The meatballs will last at least three months in the freezer.

How Much to Feed?

The quantity of food you feed your pet is highly individualistic. There are many things to take into consideration: the size, breed, and build of your pet; whether your pet is spayed or neutered; his or her activity level; the quality of the food in general; your pet's temperament, personality, and age; and even the weather and climate. But here are general feeding rules.

If you are feeding a more-concentrated, mostly meat meal, you should feed a little less than if you are feeding a meal with grain in it. If your pet's weight is about 10 to 20 pounds, (4.5 to 9 kg) about ¼ to ½ cup (56 to 112 g) of meat per day would be a good place to start. If your pet is around 40 to 60 pounds (18 to 27 kg), then about 1½ cups (337 g) of meat per day would probably work well. If your pet is around 80 to 100 pounds (36 to 45 kg), then try about 2 cups (450 g) of meat per day. Note that these would be split up into two meals so each meal would contain half the amount of meat suggested here.

Most of the recipes include quantity guidelines for feeding, but again, do not feel compelled to use them as a hard rule.

Mélange Meals versus Pure and Simple Meals

The recipes are separated into two main categories: Mélange Meals and Pure and Simple Meals. Mélange Meals are more complex in their amount of ingredients. The Pure and Simple Meals are simpler recipes using fewer ingredients and are usually faster to prepare. Although the Pure and Simple Meals may seem less balanced, remember that you are working toward a week or month of variation. You want your pet to experience some complex mixes, some simple combinations of whole ingredients, some cooked food, some grains, and various combinations of meat sources and vegetables. By providing this variation, you are ensuring that your pet gets a full array of health-giving nutrients.

You will see that many of the recipes are Pure and Simple Meal recipes. The reason I've included so many is because you should be using them as your variations to the Mélange Meals. But start with the Mélange Meal recipes, and choose three or four that appeal the most to you. Then plan your week's meals around those choices. For example, plan to serve a Mélange Meal recipe on Monday evening, Tuesday evening, Wednesday morning, Thursday evening, and Sunday morning. Fill in the rest of the meals (if you are doing two a day, it would be nine other meals) with selections from the Pure and Simple recipes.

There are a number of raw and cooked and grain and grainless options for each category of meal. Although most of the recipes are for both cats and dogs, some are labeled Cats Only or Dogs Only, and some are labeled Whole Household, which are meals humans can share with their pets.

Ground Chicken Dinner with Seasonal Vegetables

3 pounds (1.5 kg) chicken necks

1 pound (0.4 kg) ground chicken meat

½ pound (50 g) chicken organ meats (livers, hearts, and/or gizzards) or, for feeding a cat, use up to 1 pound (100 g) of organ meats

1 cup (120 g) seasonal vegetables (any combination of carrots, zucchini, turnips, cabbage, beets, broccoli, cooked sweet potato, cooked winter squash, green beans, apples, berries, etc.)

¼ cup (7 g) ground, fresh, dark leafy greens (any combination of kale, spinach, lettuce, chard, parsley, escarole, chicory, dandelion, collards, etc.)

1 clove fresh garlic

½ cup (73 g) sunflower seeds

2 or 3 eggs

¼ cup (56 g) tahini

2 tablespoons (40 g) honey

2 tablespoons (3 g) dried parsley

2 tablespoons (6 g) dried oregano

2 tablespoons (14 g) turmeric powder

1 tablespoon (10 g) kelp

1 tablespoon (3.5 g) dulse

This is the meal I make the most for my dogs. You can skip the last five ingredients in the list and instead add Herb and Spice Healthy Supplement Powder (see page 69) right before serving.

Alternate putting the necks and organ meats and vegetables, garlic, and sunflower seeds through a meat grinder and into a large bowl. Add the remaining ingredients to the bowl and mix thoroughly. Store in a well-sealed container in the refrigerator. If you make more than can be consumed in 5 days, separate into serving-size portions and freeze. Or you can make a really big batch, and roll the mixture into serving-size meatballs and freeze them in a single layer on a baking sheet. Once frozen, put the meatballs into freezer bags for easy storing. Defrost the desired number of meatballs in the refrigerator a few days before you need them. Meatballs will last at least 3 months in the freezer.

 Serving: Feed ¼ cup (50 g) twice a day to a medium-size cat; 1 cup (200 g) twice a day to a medium-size dog.

Note: *Chicken necks can come with or without skin on them. The skin adds fat. It would be best if you used half with skin and half without skin. If you can get only chicken necks with skins, then do not add the tahini; if you can get only chicken necks without skins, be sure to use the tahini. If all the necks have skin, use white meat ground chicken; if the necks are skinless or half and half, then use dark meat ground chicken.*

 Variations: This recipe has a lot of room for variation—just don't get carried away with adding different vegetables and end up feeding your pet more veggies than meat. You want to keep at least a 4:1 ratio of meat to vegetables, or even better, 5:1.

Chicken Neck and Turkey Dinner with Seasonal Vegetables

6 pounds (3 kg) chicken necks

1 pound (455 g) chicken organ meats (livers, hearts, and/or gizzards)

2 cups (240 g) seasonal produce (any combination of carrots, zucchini, turnips, cabbage, beets, broccoli, cooked sweet potato, cooked winter squash, green beans, apples, berries, etc.)

1 clove garlic

½ cup (60 g) walnuts

2 pounds (910 g) ground turkey meat, preferably dark

½ cup (15 g) finely chopped fresh dark, leafy greens* (any combination of kale, spinach, lettuce, chard, parsley, escarole, chicory, dandelion, collards, etc.)

5 eggs

¼ cup (60 g) tahini

2 tablespoons (40 g) honey

2 tablespoons (3 g) dried parsley

2 tablespoons (6 g) dried oregano

2 tablespoons (14 g) turmeric powder

1 tablespoon (10 g) kelp

1 tablespoon (3.5 g) dulse

*Or process through the meat grinder, alternating with other ingredients.

This is another favorite meal in my house. You can skip the last five ingredients in the list and instead add Herb and Spice Healthy Supplement Powder (see page 69) right before serving.

Alternate putting the necks, organ meats, produce, garlic, and walnuts through a meat grinder and into a large bowl. Add the remaining ingredients to the bowl and mix thoroughly. Store in a well-sealed container in the refrigerator. If you made more than can be consumed in 5 days, separate into serving-size portions and freeze.

 Serving: Feed ¼ cup (50 g) twice a day to a medium-size cat; 1 cup (200 g) twice a day to a medium-size dog.

Note: *See the note about chicken necks in Ground Chicken Dinner with Seasonal Vegetables on page 90.*

Ground Chicken Necks and Beef Mash with Seasonal Vegetables

Mixing in some ground beef offers a nice variation, and the bones in the ground chicken necks provide the necessary balance of calcium for the meat. You can skip the last five ingredients in the list and instead add Herb and Spice Healthy Supplement Powder (see page 69) right before serving.

Alternate putting the necks, organ meats, and produce through a meat grinder and into a large bowl. Add the remaining ingredients to the bowl and mix thoroughly. Store in a well-sealed container in the refrigerator. If you made more than can be consumed in 5 days, separate into serving-size portions and freeze.

 Serving: Feed ¼ cup (50 g) twice a day to a medium-size cat; 1 cup (200 g) twice a day to a medium-size dog.

Note: *Oregano is an herb rich in antioxidants and phytonutrients, great for optimizing and strengthening your pet's immune system.*

 Variations: You can substitute ground lamb for the ground beef in this recipe, or combine lamb and beef.

2 pounds (910 g) chicken necks (preferably1 pound [455 g] with skin and 1 pound [455 g] without skin)

½ pound (227 g) chicken livers and hearts or, for feeding a cat, up to **1 pound (455 g) organ meats**

1½ cups (180 g) seasonal produce (any combination of carrots, zucchini, turnips, cabbage, beets, broccoli, cooked sweet potato, cooked winter squash, green beans, apples, berries, etc.)

1 pound (455 g) ground chicken meat (if all necks have skin, use white meat; if necks are skinless or half and half, use dark meat)

2 pounds (910 g) ground beef (85 percent lean)

⅓ cup (10 g) finely chopped fresh dark, leafy greens* (any combination of kale, spinach, lettuce, chard, parsley, escarole, chicory, dandelion, collards, etc.)

3 or **4 eggs**

2 tablespoons (40 g) honey

2 tablespoons (3 g) dried parsley

2 tablespoons (6 g) dried oregano

2 tablespoons (14 g) turmeric powder

1 tablespoon (10 g) kelp

1 tablespoon (3.5 g) dulse

*Or process through the meat grinder, alternating with other ingredients.

Ground Frozen Fish Mash with Seasonal Vegetables

2 pounds (910 g) frozen fish fillets
(keep frozen, but you may
have to cut into strips to fit into
your meat grinder; leave any
skins on)

½ pound (227 g) organ meats
(livers, hearts, gizzards)

½ cup (60 g) seasonal produce
(any combination of carrots,
zucchini, turnips, cabbage,
beets, broccoli, cooked sweet
potato, cooked winter squash,
green beans, apples, berries,
etc.)

½ cup (67 g) pumpkin seeds

**¼ cup (7 g) finely chopped
fresh dark, leafy greens*** (any
combination of kale, spinach,
lettuce, chard, parsley,
escarole, chicory, dandelion,
collards, etc.)

1 or **2 eggs**

2 tablespoons (6 g) dried dill

1 tablespoon (3 g) dried oregano

**1 tablespoon (7 g) turmeric
powder**

1 tablespoon (6 g) anise or
fennel powder

1 tablespoon (10 g) kelp

*Or process through the meat
grinder, alternating with other
ingredients.

You could also mix chicken necks and fish fillets as an alternative meal option.

Alternate putting the fish, organ meats, produce, and pumpkin seeds through a meat grinder and into a large bowl. Add the remaining ingredients to the bowl and mix thoroughly. Store in a well-sealed container in the refrigerator. If you made more than can be consumed in 3 days, separate into serving-size portions and freeze.

 Serving: Feed ¼ cup (50 g) twice a day to a medium-size cat; 1 cup (200 g) twice a day to a medium-size dog.

Note: *Frozen fish fillets are a convenient alternative to using chicken necks. I mostly use frozen whiting or mackerel fillets, but any frozen fish fillets would work. I like the oiliness of the whiting and mackerel—they're both very high in EPA and DHA omega-3 fatty acids. Don't thaw the fillets because they grind much more effectively when frozen.*

 Variations: This recipe has a lot of room for variation— just don't get carried away with adding too many vegetables and end up feeding your pet more veggies than meat. You want to keep at least a 4:1 ratio of meat to vegetables, or even better, 5:1.

Turkey with Millet, Fennel, and Tahini

This recipe combines some unusual flavors, which are great for providing variation. Start with a small batch—some cats and dogs may find the flavors too unusual, but others love them! This dinner usually has a calming effect on the pets in my household.

In a large bowl, mix all of the ingredients together thoroughly.

 Serving: Feed about ⅓ cup (67 g) twice a day to a medium-size cat; 1½ cups (300 g) twice a day to a medium-size dog.

Note: *Turkey is a calming food. I usually recommend it for animals that are skinny and overly energetic. If you have a rather sedentary and overweight pet, I would suggest substituting chicken for the turkey.*

 Variations: You can substitute 1 pound (455 g) of the ground turkey with ground turkey necks and eliminate the bonemeal. Use 1½ pounds (682 g) of ground turkey necks and 1 pound (455 g) of plain ground turkey meat.

3 pounds (1.5 kg) ground turkey (preferably dark meat)

3 cups (555 g) cooked millet (follow package directions)

3 eggs

½ cup (120 g) tahini paste

1 cup (130 g) cooked carrots

¼ cup (26 g) raw minced fennel bulb

3 tablespoons (27 g) bonemeal

2 tablespoons (3 g) dried parsley

2 tablespoons (14 g) turmeric powder

Polenta and Salmon

2 cups (314 g) cooked polenta

3 cans (14.75 ounces, or 418 g each) wild pink Alaskan salmon

1 cup (225 g) raw chopped chicken hearts

1 cup (130 g) cooked carrots

¼ cup (7 g) finely chopped fresh dark, leafy greens* (any combination of kale, spinach, lettuce, chard, parsley, escarole, chicory, dandelion, collards, etc.)

3 tablespoons (27 g) bonemeal

2 tablespoons (3 g) dried parsley

2 tablespoons (14 g) turmeric powder

1 tablespoon (6 g) aniseed or fennel seed powder

1 tablespoon (10 g) kelp

1 tablespoon (3.5 g) dulse

*Or process through the meat grinder, alternating with other ingredients.

Cats can be a bit finicky about grains, but they do seem to truly enjoy this fishy polenta. You can skip the last five ingredients in the list and instead add Herb and Spice Healthy Supplement Powder (see page 69) right before serving.

In a large bowl, mix all ingredients together thoroughly. Store in a well-sealed container in the refrigerator.

 Serving: Feed about ⅓ cup (67 g) twice a day to a medium-size cat; 1½ cups (300 g) twice a day to a medium-size dog.

Note: *Polenta is cornmeal. You can make it with water, but it comes out tastier and more nutritious if you make it with stock.*

 Variations: You can use canned jack mackerel instead of salmon.

Polenta and Chicken

3 pounds (1.5 kg) chicken necks

1 pound (455 g) raw chicken hearts

½ pound (227 g) raw chicken livers

1 cup (120 g) seasonal produce (any combination of carrots, zucchini, turnips, cabbage, beets, broccoli, cooked sweet potato, cooked winter squash, green beans, apples, berries)

¼ cup (27 g) pecans

1 pound (455 g) ground chicken meat

4 cups (628 g) cooked polenta

¼ cup (7 g) finely chopped fresh dark, leafy greens* (any combination of kale, spinach, lettuce, chard, parsley, escarole, chicory, dandelion, collards, etc.)

1 can (14.75 ounces, or 418 g) wild pink Alaskan salmon

2 tablespoons (3 g) dried parsley

2 tablespoons (14 g) turmeric powder

1 tablespoon (6 g) aniseed or fennel seed powder

1 tablespoon (10 g) kelp

1 tablespoon (3.5 g) dulse

*Or process through the meat grinder, alternating with other ingredients.

I tend to feed a small percentage of my meals with grains in them, but I do want to also make an effort to provide variety. If your pet exhibits sensitivities or allergies to grains, don't use them. But many pets, especially dogs, do fine with grains in their diets. Just make sure you are feeding more meat than grain overall. You can skip the last five ingredients in the list and instead add Herb and Spice Healthy Supplement Powder (see page 69) right before serving.

Alternate putting the necks, organ meats, produce, and pecans through a meat grinder and into a large bowl. Add the remaining ingredients to the bowl and mix thoroughly. Store in a well-sealed container in the refrigerator. If you made more than can be consumed in 5 days, separate into serving-size portions and freeze.

 Serving: Feed about ⅓ cup (67 g) twice a day to a medium-size cat; 1½ cups (300 g) twice a day to a medium-size dog.

Note: *See the note about chicken necks in Ground Chicken Dinner with Seasonal Vegetables on page 90.*

 Variations: This recipe has a lot of room for variation—just don't get carried away with adding different vegetables and end up feeding your pet more veggies than meat. You want to keep at least a 4:1 ratio of meat to vegetables, or even better, 5:1.

Veggie Oat and Chicken Dinner

This is basically the same as the Ground Chicken Dinner with Seasonal Vegetables on page 90, but with The Ultimate Veggie Oats (see page 102) added. Because this recipe has grains, I'd feed a bit more than the grainless version, but it is still an effective way to stretch your pet food budget. You can skip the last five ingredients in the list and instead add Herb and Spice Healthy Supplement Powder (see page 69) right before serving.

Alternate putting the chicken necks, organ meats, produce, garlic, and sunflower seeds through a meat grinder and into a large bowl. Add the remaining ingredients to the bowl and mix thoroughly. Store in a well-sealed container in the refrigerator. If you made more than can be consumed in 5 days, separate into serving-size portions and freeze.

I usually make a really big batch, starting with 40 pounds (18 kg) of chicken necks. Then I roll the ground mixture into serving-size meatballs and freeze them in a single layer on a baking sheet. Once frozen, I put the meatballs into freezer bags for easy storing. Then I just defrost the meatballs I need in the refrigerator a few days before I use them. Meatballs will last at least 3 months in the freezer.

 Serving: Feed ⅓ cup (67 g) twice a day to a medium-size cat; 1½ cups (300 g) twice a day to a medium-size dog.

Note: *See the note about chicken necks in Ground Chicken Dinner with Seasonal Vegetables on page 90.*

- 3 pounds (1.5 kg) chicken necks
- ½ pound (227 g) chicken organ meats (livers, hearts, and/or gizzards) or, for feeding a cat, up to 1 pound (455 g) organ meats
- 1 cup (120 g) seasonal produce (any combination of carrots, zucchini, turnips, cabbage, beets, broccoli, cooked sweet potato, cooked winter squash, green beans, apples, berries, etc.)
- 1 clove garlic
- ½ cup (67 g) sunflower seeds
- 1 pound (455 g) ground chicken meat
- ¼ cup (7 g) finely chopped fresh dark, leafy greens* (any combination of kale, spinach, lettuce, chard, parsley, escarole, chicory, dandelion, collards, etc.)
- 2 to 3 eggs
- ¼ cup (60 g) tahini
- 2 tablespoons (40 g) honey
- 6 cups (1200 g) cooked Ultimate Veggie Oats
- 2 tablespoons (3 g) dried parsley
- 2 tablespoons (6 g) dried oregano
- 2 tablespoons (14 g) turmeric powder
- 1 tablespoon (10 g) kelp
- 1 tablespoon (3.5 g) dulse

*Or process through the meat grinder, alternating with other ingredients.

Beef, Sardines, and Polenta

4 cups (628 g) cooked polenta

3 pounds (1.4 kg) ground beef

1 pound (455 g) raw chopped
chicken hearts

2 cans (3.5 ounces, or 100 g
each) sardines

1 cup (130 g) cooked carrots

¼ cup (7 g) finely chopped
fresh dark, leafy greens* (any
combination of kale, spinach,
lettuce, chard, parsley,
escarole, chicory, dandelion,
collards, etc.)

3 tablespoons (27 g) bonemeal

2 tablespoons (3 g) dried parsley

2 tablespoons (14 g) turmeric
powder

1 tablespoon (6 g) aniseed or
fennel seed powder

1 tablespoon (10 g) kelp

1 tablespoon (3.5 g) dulse

*Or process through the meat
grinder, alternating with other
ingredients.

This is a lovely meal—full of nutrients—
and it smells really good if the polenta
is still warm as you mix it together. If it
weren't for the raw meat and hearts, I'd be
tempted to eat it myself! You can skip the
last five ingredients in the list and instead
add Herb and Spice Healthy Supplement
Powder (see page 69) right before serving.

In a large bowl, mix all the ingredients together thoroughly.
Store in a well-sealed container in the refrigerator. If you made
more than can be consumed in 5 days, separate into serving-
size portions and freeze.

 Serving: Feed about ⅓ cup (67 g) twice a day to
a medium-size cat; 1½ cups (300 g) twice a day to a
medium-size dog.

Note: *See the note about chicken necks in Ground Chicken
Dinner with Seasonal Vegetables on page 90.*

 Variations: This recipe has a lot of room for variation—
just don't get carried away with adding different vegetables and end up feeding your pet more veggies than
meat. You want to keep at least a 4:1 ratio of meat to
vegetables, or even better, 5:1.

Beef and Veggie Patties

Like the Lamb and Salmon Patties with Wild Greens on page 141, you can choose not to cook these burgers and just serve them raw to your pets.

In a large bowl, combine the beef, egg, bonemeal, kelp, garlic, and produce until well mixed. Add a little stock or water if the mixture is too dry to hold together to form patties. For a cat or small dog, form patties a little less than ½-inch (1.25-cm) thick and about 2 inches (5 cm) in diameter. For larger dogs, make hamburger-size patties.

Heat the olive oil in a skillet over medium heat. Place the patties in the skillet; they should sizzle. Cook about 2 minutes on each side for small patties and 4 minutes on each side for hamburger-size patties. They will still be rare in the center, and smell very tasty.

 Serving: Feed 1 or 2 small patties twice a day to a medium-size cat or small dog; 1 large patty twice a day to a medium-size dog.

Note: *Because you are using raw vegetables, it is important that they are fully minced. A food processor will do the job quickly.*

 Variations: Substitute ground turkey for the ground beef. You can add ¼ cup (32 g) ground pine nuts to this recipe.

2 cups (450 g) ground beef

1 egg

2 tablespoons (18 g) bonemeal

2 teaspoons kelp

1 teaspoon granulated or **powdered garlic**

½ cup (60 g) minced raw produce (any combination of carrots, zucchini, beets, broccoli, kale, cauliflower, sweet potato, winter squash, green beans, apples, etc.)

Chicken stock or **water**

2 tablespoons (30 ml) olive oil

The Ultimate Veggie Oats

Water or stock

1 beet, coarsely chopped

About 1 cup (67 g) chopped kale leaves

About ½ cup (45 g) chopped green or **purple cabbage**

Oats, rolled or **steel cut**, enough to make 6 cups (480 g) cooked

My original batches of Veggie Oats were made from leftover water after I boiled beets. I would take the beets out of the water and just dump some rolled oats in to cook in the red-colored beet water. I liked that the oats would soak up the nutrients that came out of the beets.

Start by looking at the directions for cooking the oats. Determine how much liquid you need, then add 1½ cups (355 ml) more water or stock than the directions call for and put all the liquid into a large pot.

Bring the liquid to a boil and add the beet, kale, and cabbage. Reduce the heat to medium and partially cover. Let simmer about ½ hour, or until the vegetables are soft. Add the oats and cook as directed on the package. Let cool to room temperature before feeding or adding to raw meat mixes.

 Serving: Veggie Oats are best for dogs; cats may find this meal too grainy. I like to use it as a side dish to a meatier meal or as an additional ingredient to a recipe. By itself, don't feed more than about 1 cup (200 g) twice a day to a medium-size dog. As a side dish, you can substitute about ¼ to ⅓ of the main meat meal with veggie oats for your dog. If your cat likes oats, you can substitute or add about 1 Tbsp (12 g) to your cat's main meat meal. If you have some left over, it can be frozen for future use.

 Variations: You can use any animal-based stock for this recipe—chicken, turkey, beef, fish. They all work great and provide different sets of nutrients. And while oats are quick and easy, you can prepare this recipe using barley or brown rice instead of the oats.

Chicken Stock

Chicken stock is a wonderful food. You can feed it as stock to your cat or dog as a meal, use it to cook grains for your cat or dog instead of using water, or use it to build a full chicken soup meal.

In a stockpot, combine all ingredients and cover with cold water. Bring to a boil, partially cover, and let simmer for at least 3 to 5 hours, or all day. While it is simmering, stir and break up the carcass and vegetables with a wooden spoon; skim off any impurities or foam. Keep an eye on the water level and add a cup or two (235 to 475 ml) of water if necessary. Don't let the stock boil vigorously; keep it at a gentle simmer. Strain while still quite hot, and discard bones and other solids. You can then directly feed this stock once cooled, or use it in another recipe, or store it in the freezer for use at another time.

 Serving: As a porridge-style single meal, feed about ⅓ cup (67 g) twice a day to a medium-size cat; 1½ cups (300 g) twice a day to a medium-size dog.

Note: *The chickens you buy in most stores these days are grown quickly and don't make a very flavorful stock. At certain farms you can buy "soup" chickens, sometimes referred to as "fowl," which are basically older chickens, and they make a great soup. To get more flavor from regular chickens, you can roast the chicken first, remove most of the meat, and then use the leftover carcass bones for your stock. This makes a very flavorful soup and gives you meat to either eat as a regular roast chicken meal, or to save and put back into the soup you make from the stock. Also note that you can use any poultry for this recipe.*

(Continued)

1 whole chicken or leftover carcass bones from a roasted chicken

3 or **4 stalks celery** (can include leaves)

3 or **4 carrots, broken up** (wash, but leave skins on)

6 cloves garlic*

Black pepper

Sprinkling of sea salt

Bay leaf

Handful of parsley sprigs or **dried parsley**

Thyme sprigs or **dried thyme**

*You can add more garlic, or dried mushrooms, cayenne pepper, astragalus root slices, oregano, fennel seeds, or sprigs of other fresh herbs such as lovage, borage, chives, tarragon, etc. You can be creative with a chicken stock.

Chicken Stock

 Variations: Sometimes I add barley (or rice will work as well) to the chicken soup to give it more of a porridge consistency. Once strained, this can be used to make chicken soup for your animals. I like to make it thick with meat and vegetables for them, as I find most cats and dogs don't like to fish around in broth; they prefer to drink broth and chomp up solid food.

Simply add cooked pieces of chicken meat or raw, ground chicken, turkey, or beef to the hot broth. Let the flavor meld a bit, and add cooked carrots and/or other vegetables. You'll be adding solid food to the broth in

Meaty Bones Stock

Like the Chicken Stock on page 105, this is best used as either a straight broth that your pet can drink, or made into a porridge-like consistency. You can also use the stock to cook vegetables or grains instead of using water, imparting a gamut of nutrients.

Preheat oven to 350°F (180° C, or gas mark 4). Place the bones in a large roasting pan. Drizzle ¼ cup (60 ml) of the olive oil over them; add the tomato paste and wine or vinegar. Rub to coat the bones thoroughly. Add pepper to taste and a dash of salt. Roast for 30 minutes. Meanwhile, clean and cut up the carrots, celery, garlic, and parsnip. In a large bowl, toss the vegetables with the remaining ¼ cup (60 ml) olive oil. After the bones have roasted for 30 minutes, add the vegetables to the roasting pan, mix well, and roast for another 30 minutes, or until nicely browned. Remove from the oven.

Dump the bones and vegetables into a big stockpot and cover with water. Add the pepper, thyme, bay leaves, parsley, and tomatoes.

Bring slowly to a simmer, stirring often and skimming off impurities as they rise to the top. You will need to let this broth simmer for about 12 hours. Keep the lid ajar. Strain while the stock is warm, let it cool down, and refrigerate. Discard the cooked bones and bay leaves. (You can use the carrots and other cooked veggies and pieces of meat.) Use stock as is, to cook grains or vegetables, or to make a thick soup or a beef porridge.

 Serving: As a porridge-style single meal, feed about ⅓ cup (67 g) twice a day to a medium-size cat; 1½ cups (300 g) twice a day to a medium-size dog.

(Continued)

About 5 pounds (2.3 kg) soup bones from grass-fed organic beef*

½ cup (120 ml) olive oil, divided

1 can (6 ounces, or 170 g) tomato paste

½ cup (120 ml) red wine or red wine vinegar

¼ teaspoon pepper

Dash of salt

2 carrots

2 stalks celery

6 cloves garlic

1 parsnip

Several sprigs fresh thyme or 1 teaspoon dried thyme

4 bay leaves

1 bunch fresh parsley

1 can (15 ounces, or 425 g) diced tomatoes

*Use a selection of bones from around the animal for the most nutritional variety. I try to use both jointy (leg/marrow) bones, rich in glucosamine, and ribby bones in each batch.

Meaty Bones Stock

 Variations: You can make this recipe with beef, lamb, goat, or venison. I like to make it thick with meat and vegetables for my cats and dogs, because I find they don't like to fish around in broth; they prefer to either drink broth or chomp up solid food.

To make a thick soup, simply add cooked pieces of chicken meat or raw, ground chicken, turkey, or beef to the hot stock. Let the flavors meld a bit, and add cooked carrots and/or other vegetables. Add solid food to the stock in about a 2:1 ratio.

To make a porridge, simply add cooked grains until the consistency is oatmeal-like. I find barley and brown rice work very well for this.

"Essentials" Dinner

Feed your pet this dinner twice a week, and your cat or dog will get the full array of essential omega-3s and amino acids.

In a large bowl, mix all the ingredients together thoroughly.

 Serving: Feed ¼ cup (50 g) twice a day to a medium-size cat; 1 cup (200 g) twice a day to a medium-size dog.

 Variations: You can add 1 part cooked grain to 1 part meat. Another variation is to use a beef heart instead of chicken hearts, and double the amount of the other ingredients: 1 minced beef heart, 2 cans salmon, and 2 eggs.

1 can (14.75 ounces, or 418 g) wild pink Alaskan salmon

½ to 1 pound (227 to 455 g) raw chicken hearts, chopped

1 egg

Beef Chunks with Nuts and Seeds

1 cup (95 g) ground nuts (can be a combination of walnuts, sunflower seeds, and pumpkin seeds)

6 eggs

¼ cup (7 g) finely chopped fresh dark, leafy greens (any combination of kale, spinach, lettuce, chard, parsley, escarole, chicory, dandelion, collards, etc.)

2 tablespoons (30 g) tahini

2 tablespoons (18 g) bonemeal

2 pounds (910 g) raw stew beef

As noted before, cats usually prefer ground meat to chunks, and you can easily substitute ground beef for the chunks in this recipe. The ground meat and eggs will help you gracefully hide the nuts and greens for finicky cats.

In a large bowl, combine the nuts, eggs, greens, tahini, and bonemeal and mix thoroughly. Add the beef chunks and toss until evenly coated with the egg and nut mixture.

 Serving: Feed ¼ cup (50 g) twice a day to a medium-size cat; 1 cup (200 g) twice a day to a medium-size dog.

 Variations: Replace the beef with lamb stew meat.

Beef Chunks with Chicken Necks and Eggs

2 pounds (910 g) chicken necks
(1 pound [455 g] with skin and
1 pound [455 g] without)

1 cup (120 g) seasonal produce
(any combination of carrots,
zucchini, turnips, cabbage,
beets, broccoli, cooked sweet
potato, cooked winter squash,
green beans, apples, berries,
etc.)

1 pound (455 g) raw stew beef

6 eggs

Cats usually prefer ground meat to chunks, and you can easily substitute ground beef for the chunks in this recipe.

Alternate putting the necks and produce through a meat grinder and into a large bowl. Add the beef chunks and eggs to the bowl and mix thoroughly.

 Serving: Feed ¼ cup (50 g) twice a day to a medium-size cat; 1 cup (200 g) twice a day to a medium-size dog.

 Variations: You can add a scoop of The Ultimate Veggie Oats (see page 102) to this meal. I sometimes sprinkle dried oregano, stinging nettle, and kelp/dulse into the oats to give an extra health boost.

Soft-Boiled Eggs, Baked Carrots, and Ground Chicken

Soft-boiling the eggs leaves the yolks runny and more raw. Raw egg yolk is very healthy for your pet.

Preheat oven to 350°F (180°C, or gas mark 4). Wash and trim the carrots and place in a small oiled or buttered baking dish. Bake for about 20 to 25 minutes, or until soft and lightly browned. Let cool. Transfer to a large bowl.

Peel and chop the eggs, and add to the bowl with the carrots. With a fork, mash the carrots and break up the eggs. Add the ground chicken and bonemeal and combine.

 Serving: Feed ¼ cup (50 g) twice a day to a medium-size cat; 1 cup (200 g) twice a day to a medium-size dog.

4 carrots

3 soft-boiled eggs

1 pound (455 g) ground chicken meat, preferably dark

1 tablespoon (9 g) bonemeal

Big Baked Veggies and Soft-Boiled Eggs

2 beets

1 sweet potato

1 small butternut squash

2 tablespoons (30 ml) olive oil

3 tablespoons (7 g) minced fresh herbs or 2 tablespoons (4 g) dried mixed herbs (rosemary, thyme, mint, sage, oregano, and/or marjoram, etc.)

12 soft-boiled eggs

3 pounds (1.5 kg) ground chicken meat, preferably dark

2 cans (14.75 ounces, or 418 g each) wild pink Alaskan salmon

1 tablespoon (9 g) bonemeal

This recipe is very similar to the Soft-Boiled Eggs, Baked Carrots, and Ground Chicken recipe on page 113, but provides even more well-rounded variation to your pet's diet. I really love to serve this meal during the winter.

Preheat oven to 350°F (180°C, or gas mark 4). Wash, peel, and cut up the beets, sweet potato, and butternut squash into similarly sized pieces, about 1 inch (2.5 cm). Place in a small oiled or buttered baking dish, and toss with the remaining olive oil, about 1 tablespoon (15 ml). Bake for 20 to 25 minutes, or until soft and lightly browned. Let cool, mash up, and mix in the herbs.

Peel and chop the eggs. Place in a large bowl with the ground chicken, salmon, and bonemeal. Gently stir in the mashed, baked vegetables.

 Serving: Feed ¼ cup (50 g) twice a day to a medium-size cat; 1 cup (200 g) twice a day to a medium-size dog.

Big Baked Veggies and Lamb Chunks

Big Baked Veggies are quite sweet, and a big favorite of my animals. The veggies will also add a full gamut of antioxidants to your pets' meals.

Preheat oven to 350°F (180°C, or gas mark 4). Wash, peel, and cut up the beets, sweet potato, and butternut squash into similarly sized pieces, about 1 inch (2.5 cm). Place in a small oiled or buttered baking dish, and toss with the remaining olive oil, about 1 tablespoon (15 ml). Bake for 20 to 25 minutes, or until soft and lightly browned. Let cool, mash up, and mix in the herbs.

In a large bowl, mix the lamb chunks, sardines, and bonemeal. Gently stir in the mashed, baked vegetables.

 Serving: Feed ¼ cup (50 g) twice a day to a medium-size cat; 1 cup (200 g) twice a day to a medium-size dog.

 Variations: Substitute beef stew meat for the lamb. If your pet doesn't do well with chunky food, use ground meat instead of stew meat.

2 beets

1 sweet potato

1 small butternut squash

2 tablespoons (30 ml) olive oil

3 tablespoons (7 g) minced fresh herbs or 2 tablespoons (4 g) dried mixed herbs (rosemary, thyme, mint, sage, oregano, and/or marjoram, etc.)

3 pounds (1.5 kg) raw lamb stew meat

1 can (3.5 ounces, or 100 g) sardines

3 tablespoons (27 g) bonemeal

Bright Celery and Cucumber Meal

2 pounds (910 g) ground turkey

1 can (3.5 ounces, or 100 g) sardines

½ cup (60 g) puréed celery

½ cup (70 g) puréed cucumber

1 tablespoon (9 g) bonemeal

1 tablespoon (4.5 g) alfalfa powder

1 teaspoon kelp

1 teaspoon dulse

Sometimes you want to make your pet a light and refreshing meal for rejuvenation and detoxification. I usually turn to celery and cucumber for creating such meals. The nutrients they supply are fabulous for cellular rejuvenation and provide a gentle cleansing quality as well.

In a large bowl, mix all of the ingredients together thoroughly.

 Serving: Feed ¼ cup (50 g) twice a day to a medium-size cat; 1 cup (200 g) twice a day to a medium-size dog.

Big Baked Veggies and Raw Chicken

2 beets

1 sweet potato

1 small butternut squash

2 tablespoons (30 ml) olive oil

3 tablespoons (7 g) minced fresh herbs or 2 tablespoons (4 g) dried mixed herbs (rosemary, thyme, mint, sage, oregano, and/or marjoram, etc.)

2 pounds (910 g) chicken necks (preferably 1 pound [455 g] with skin and 1 pound [455 g] without skin)

1 pound (455 g) ground chicken meat (white meat if chicken necks have skin; dark meat if necks are skinless or half and half)

1 tablespoon (4.5 g) alfalfa powder

I often cook up a double batch of Big Baked Veggies and then use half for feeding my family.

Preheat oven to 350°F (180°C, or gas mark 4). Wash, peel, and cut up the beets, sweet potato, and butternut squash into similarly sized pieces, about 1 inch. Place in a small oiled or buttered baking dish, and toss with the remaining olive oil, about 1 tablespoon (15 ml). Bake for 20 to 25 minutes, or until soft and lightly browned. Let cool, mash up, and mix in the herbs.

While the vegetables are baking, put the chicken necks in a meat grinder and grind into a large bowl. Add the vegetables, chicken meat, and alfalfa powder and mix well.

 Serving: Feed ¼ cup (50 g) twice a day to a medium-size cat; 1 cup (200 g) twice a day to a medium-size dog.

Turkey with Coconut Oil and Vegetables

This is a well-rounded meal; the coconut oil provides a whole new variety of fatty acids and nutrients.

In a large bowl, mix all of the ingredients together thoroughly.

 Serving: Feed about ¼ cup (50 g) twice a day to a medium-size cat; 1 cup (200 g) twice a day to a medium-size dog.

 Variations: If you aren't using dark meat turkey, add an amino acid supplement to this meal. The white meat has a very small amount of amino acids.

4 pounds (1.8 kg) ground turkey (preferably dark meat)

4 eggs

½ cup (120 ml) coconut oil

1 cup (120 g) ground raw (or cooked and mashed) **seasonal produce** (any combination of carrots, zucchini, turnips, cabbage, beets, broccoli, cooked sweet potato, cooked winter squash, green beans, apples, berries, etc.)

¼ cup (7 g) finely chopped fresh dark, leafy greens (any combination of kale, spinach, lettuce, chard, parsley, escarole, chicory, dandelion, collards, etc.)

1 clove garlic

4 tablespoons (36 g) bonemeal

2 tablespoons (14 g) turmeric powder

1 tablespoon (10 g) kelp

1 tablespoon (3.5 g) dulse

Ground Chicken with Summer Squash

Sardines and Beef with Celery and Cucumber

This is a simple and easy recipe to pull together fast. I have found that using a wide cheese grater or mandoline makes quick work of mincing the summer squash.

2 pounds (910 g) ground chicken

2 eggs

1 pound (455 g) ground chicken hearts

1 cup (255 g) minced summer squash (zucchini, yellow squash, etc.)

1 tablespoon (9 g) bonemeal

1 tablespoon (4.5 g) alfalfa powder

1 teaspoon kelp

1 teaspoon dulse

In a large bowl, mix all of the ingredients together thoroughly.

 Serving: Feed ¼ cup (50 g) twice a day to a medium-size cat; 1 cup (200 g) twice a day to a medium-size dog.

Beef is a nice flavor change from the poultry in the Bright Celery and Cucumber Meal on page 116.

2 cans (3.5 ounces, or 100 g each) sardines

2 pounds (910 g) ground beef

½ cup (60 g) puréed celery

½ cup (70 g) puréed cucumber

1 tablespoon (9 g) bonemeal

1 tablespoon (4.5 g) alfalfa powder

1 teaspoon kelp

1 teaspoon dulse

In a large bowl, mix all of the ingredients together thoroughly.

 Serving: Feed ¼ cup (50 g) twice a day to a medium-size cat; 1 cup (200 g) twice a day to a medium-size dog.

Ground Turkey with Tahini, Cucumber, and Lettuce

Ground Turkey with Arugula

This is a good meal to make when you have leftover salad. Simply throw the salad greens, dressing and all, into a food processor with the other ingredients and grind it all up.

2 pounds (910 g) ground turkey meat

1 egg

¼ cup (60 g) tahini

½ cup (60 g) puréed cucumber

½ cup (15 g) minced lettuce leaves

1 tablespoon (9 g) bonemeal

1 tablespoon (4.5 g) alfalfa powder

1 teaspoon kelp

1 teaspoon dulse

1 teaspoon granulated or powdered garlic

In a large bowl, mix all of the ingredients together thoroughly.

 Serving: Feed ¼ cup (50 g) twice a day to a medium-size cat; 1 cup (200 g) twice a day to a medium-size dog.

Arugula may be too flavorful for some cats, but dogs tend to love it. If the strong arugula flavor seems to be too much, try adding other greens such as dandelion, chicory, endive, or escarole.

3 pounds (1.5 kg) ground turkey meat

½ pound (227 g) ground organ meats

2 eggs

1 cup (30 g) minced arugula

1 tablespoon (9 g) bonemeal

In a large bowl, mix all of the ingredients together thoroughly.

 Serving: Feed ¼ cup (50 g) twice a day to a medium-size cat; 1 cup (200 g) twice a day to a medium-size dog.

Purple Berry Meat

2 pounds (910 g) chicken necks, (preferably 1 pound [455 g] with skin and 1 pound [455 g] without skin)

1 cup (145 g) berries (any combination of blueberries, raspberries, strawberries, blackberries, etc.)

1 pound (455 g) ground chicken meat (if necks have skin, use white meat; if necks are skinless or half and half, use dark meat)

¼ cup (7 g) finely chopped fresh dark, leafy greens* (any combination of kale, spinach, lettuce, chard, parsley, escarole, chicory, dandelion, collards, etc.)

*Or process through the meat grinder, alternating with other ingredients.

I love making this recipe. It is so festive and just bursting with nutrients! The berries provide your pet with some of the most powerful antioxidants available.

Alternate putting the necks and berries through a meat grinder and into a large bowl. Add the remaining ingredients to the bowl and mix thoroughly.

 Serving: Feed ¼ cup (50 g) twice a day to a medium-size cat; 1 cup (200 g) twice a day to a medium-size dog.

Note: *Although fresh is best, you can use frozen berries for this recipe.*

Sweet Rose Chicken

This is a great recipe for adding variety to your pet's diet. It's bright rose-colored red and sweetened with honey, which is a powerful super food packed with all sorts of important nutrients, minerals, and micro-nutrients. Honey is an energizer and promotes healing and blood purification.

Alternate putting the necks, berries, and beets through a meat grinder and into a large bowl. Add the remaining ingredients to the bowl and mix thoroughly. Make sure the honey gets evenly integrated.

 Serving: Feed ¼ cup (50 g) twice a day to a medium-size cat; 1 cup (200 g) twice a day to a medium-size dog.

 Variations: For an extra nutritional punch, add a raw egg or some ground nuts while mixing.

2 pounds (910 g) chicken necks, (preferably 1 pound [455 g] with skin and 1 pound [455 g] without skin)

1 cup (145 g) fresh or **frozen strawberries** and/or **raspberries**

3 medium beets, cut into strips to fit easily into grinder

1 pound (455 g) ground chicken meat (if necks have skin, use white meat; if necks are skinless or half and half, use dark meat)

¼ cup (7 g) finely chopped fresh dark, leafy greens* (any combination of kale, spinach, lettuce, chard, parsley, escarole, chicory, dandelion, collards, etc.)

½ cup (160 g) honey

*Or process through the meat grinder, alternating with other ingredients.

Chicken and Baked Winter Squash with Organ Meats

1 small butternut, acorn, delicata, kuri, or **other winter squash**

2 pounds (910 g) chicken necks (preferably 1 pound [455 g] with skin and 1 pound [455 g] without skin)

1 pound (455 g) organ meats

1 pound (455 g) ground chicken meat (if all necks have skin, use white meat; if necks are skinless or half and half, use dark meat)

¼ cup (7 g) finely chopped fresh dark, leafy greens* (any combination of kale, spinach, lettuce, chard, parsley, escarole, chicory, dandelion, collards, etc.)

*Or process through the meat grinder, alternating with other ingredients.

Winter squash are usually well loved by my pets. They are sweet and full of important antioxidants. This recipe makes a nice winter-season meal.

Preheat oven to 350°F (180°C, or gas mark 4). Cut the squash in half. Place the halves skin-side-up on a baking sheet and bake for 1 to 1½ hours (depending on the size of the squash), or until the skin starts to blister and caramelize. Let the squash cool, then scoop out the flesh and pass it through a meat grinder as you grind the chicken necks and organ meats into a large bowl. Add the remaining ingredients to the bowl and mix thoroughly.

 Serving: Feed ¼ cup (50 g) twice a day to a medium-size cat; 1 cup (200 g) twice a day to a medium-size dog.

Zucchini and Pumpkin Seed Mash with Chicken Necks

It is a good idea to make sure to include a recipe highlighting pumpkin seeds in your repertoire! Pumpkin seeds are a fabulous source of fatty acids and also have the added benefit of being effective vermicides, cleansing out the intestinal tract.

Alternate putting the necks, squash, organ meats, seeds, and garlic through a meat grinder and into a large bowl. Add the ground chicken meat and alfalfa powder to the bowl and mix thoroughly.

 Serving: Feed ¼ cup (50 g) twice a day to a medium-size cat; 1 cup (200 g) twice a day to a medium-size dog.

2 pounds (910 g) chicken necks, (preferably 1 pound [455 g] with skin and 1 pound [455 g] without skin)

1 medium zucchini or other summer squash

1 pound (455 g) organ meats

½ cup (50 g) pumpkin seeds

1 clove garlic

1 pound (455 g) ground chicken meat (if necks have skin, use white meat; if necks are skinless or half and half, use dark meat)

1 tablespoon (4.5 g) alfalfa powder

Baked Sweet Potato and Chicken

2 medium sweet potatoes

2 pounds (910 g) chicken necks, (preferably 1 pound [455 g] with skin and 1 pound [455 g] without skin)

1 pound (455 g) organ meats

1 pound (455 g) ground chicken meat (if all necks have skin, use white meat; if necks are skinless or half and half, use dark meat)

¼ cup (7 g) finely chopped fresh dark, leafy greens* (any combination of kale, spinach, lettuce, chard, parsley, escarole, chicory, dandelion, collards, etc.)

1 teaspoon kelp

1 teaspoon dulse

1 teaspoon alfalfa powder

*Or process through the meat grinder, alternating with other ingredients.

I usually plan to make this recipe when I have a whole bunch of sweet potatoes. I bake them up for both this pet food recipe as well as for the whole household.

Preheat oven to 350°F (180°C, or gas mark 4). Poke the sweet potato skins on one side of each potato with a fork. Place the potatoes on a baking sheet with the fork holes facing up. Bake for about 45 minutes, or until juice is lightly leaking from them and they feel soft when poked with a fork. Remove from the oven and let cool, then scoop out the flesh and pass it through a meat grinder as you grind the chicken necks and organ meats into a large bowl. Add the remaining ingredients to the bowl and mix together thoroughly.

 Serving: Feed ¼ cup (50 g) twice a day to a medium-size cat; 1 cup (200 g) twice a day to a medium-size dog.

Baked Sweet Potato and Lamb

This is an elegant and highly nutritious meal. You can add other vegetables as well to provide additional nutrient variety.

Preheat oven to 350°F (180°C, or gas mark 4). Poke the sweet potato skins on one side of each potato with a fork. Place the potatoes on a baking sheet with the fork holes facing up. Bake for 45 minutes, or until juice is lightly leaking from them and they feel soft when poked with a fork. Remove from the oven and let cool. Scoop out the flesh into a large bowl and mix thoroughly with the remaining ingredients.

 Serving: Feed ¼ cup (50 g) twice a day to a medium-size cat; 1 cup (200 g) twice a day to a medium-size dog.

2 medium sweet potatoes

2 pounds (910 g) ground lamb

1 can (14.75 ounces, or 418 g) wild pink Alaskan salmon

1 pound (455 g) organ meats

2 tablespoons (18 g) bonemeal

2 tablespoons (9 g) alfalfa powder

1 teaspoon kelp

1 teaspoon dulse

Ground Lamb, Jack Mackerel, and Cucumber

A lovely combination of great ingredients—this is one of my cat's favorite meals besides the Sardine Salad on page 154!

2 pounds (910 g) ground lamb

1 can (14.75 ounces, or 418 g) jack mackerel

2 eggs

1 cup (135 g) puréed cucumber

¼ cup (7 g) finely chopped fresh dark, leafy greens (any combination of kale, spinach, lettuce, chard, parsley, escarole, chicory, dandelion, collards, etc.)

1 tablespoon (9 g) bonemeal

In a large bowl, mix all of the ingredients together thoroughly.

 Serving: Feed ¼ cup (50 g) twice a day to a medium-size cat; 1 cup (200 g) twice a day to a medium-size dog.

Jack Mackerel and Veggies

Here's a simple and easy meal, designed for making use of whatever vegetables you may have left over in your fridge.

2 cans (14.75 ounces, or 418 g each) jack mackerel

2 eggs

1 cup (120 g) seasonal produce (any combination of carrots, zucchini, turnips, cabbage, beets, broccoli, cooked sweet potato, cooked winter squash, green beans, apples, berries, etc.)

¼ cup (7 g) finely chopped fresh dark, leafy greens

2 tablespoons (9 g) alfalfa powder

1 teaspoon kelp

1 teaspoon dulse

1 teaspoon granulated or powdered garlic

In a large bowl, mix all of the ingredients together thoroughly.

 Serving: Feed ¼ cup (50 g) twice a day to a medium-size cat; 1 cup (200 g) twice a day to a medium-size dog.

Green Sardines

This is a fun recipe and an easy way to get some greens into finicky cats! Make sure to very finely mince the greens. You can also steam the greens lightly and then chop them, if your cat prefers. Dogs usually don't even seem to notice the greens in this meal!

4 cans (3.5 ounces, or 100 g each) sardines

1 cup (225 g) minced raw liver

1 egg

½ cup (15 g) finely chopped fresh dark, leafy greens (any combination of kale, spinach, lettuce, chard, parsley, escarole, chicory, dandelion, collards, etc.)

2 tablespoons (18 g) alfalfa powder

1 teaspoon kelp

1 teaspoon dulse

1 teaspoon granulated or **powdered garlic**

In a large bowl, mix all of the ingredients together thoroughly.

 Serving: Feed ¼ cup (50 g) twice a day to a medium-size cat; 1 cup (200 g) twice a day to a medium-size dog.

Leftover Poultry

Always give your table leftovers a quick consideration: Would any of this work for my pet's meal? Often our table leftovers can be used to add flavor or just a dash of variety to our pet food. You never want to use bone or pieces of grizzle or overcooked fat, but leftover meat can be mixed with other ingredients to make a great healthy meal.

1 to 2 cups (140 to 280 g) cooked poultry meat (remove all bones)

¼ cup (56 g) minced organ meats

1 egg

¼ cup (30 g) finely chopped raw (or cooked and mashed) **seasonal produce** (any combination of carrots, zucchini, turnips, cabbage, beets, broccoli, cooked sweet potato, cooked winter squash, green beans, apples, berries, etc.)

In a large bowl, mix all of the ingredients together thoroughly.

 Serving: Feed about ⅓ cup (67 g) twice a day to a medium-size cat; 1½ cups (300 g) twice a day to a medium-size dog.

 Variations: Add ½ to 1 cup (83 to 165 g) cooked brown rice, barley, or other grains to this meal.

Sunflower Seed Mash

Lamb and Salmon with Sunflower Seed Mash

Raw sunflower seeds have fresher oils and fats in them than roasted, but either can be used. They are extremely healthy additions to your pet food. I make an effort to integrate at least 3 or 4 meals with raw sunflower seeds into my pets' diets every month. A dash of ketchup can make this meal more savory for your pet.

1 cup (95 g) ground sunflower seeds

4 cans (3.5 ounces, or 100 g each) sardines

2 eggs

In a large bowl, mix all of the ingredients together thoroughly.

 Serving: Feed ¼ cup (50 g) twice a day to a medium-size cat; 1 cup (200 g) twice a day to a medium-size dog.

 Variations: Substitute ½ can of any other fish for each can of sardines.

This is another great combination recipe using sunflower seeds that my animals always get excited for!

1 pound (455 g) ground lamb

1 can (14.75 ounces, or 418 g) wild pink Alaskan salmon

1 cup (95 g) ground sunflower seeds

½ cup (112 g) minced organ meats

2 eggs

1 tablespoon (9 g) bonemeal

1 tablespoon (9 g) alfalfa powder

In a large bowl, mix all of the ingredients together thoroughly.

 Serving: Feed ¼ cup (50 g) twice a day to a medium-size cat; 1 cup (200 g) twice a day to a medium-size dog.

Apple Turkey

You don't need to bake the apples, although I find cats like this meal better when the apples are cooked. My dogs consider this a fun treat whether the apples are raw or baked. I also have a tendency, once I start to smell that baked apple scent, to sprinkle cinnamon on them.

2 apples (any variety)

3 pounds (1.5 kg) ground turkey meat,
preferably dark

1 egg

¼ cup (7 g) finely chopped fresh dark, leafy greens (any combination of kale, spinach, lettuce, chard, parsley, escarole, chicory, dandelion, collards, etc.)

3 tablespoons (27 g) bonemeal

Preheat oven to 350°F (180°C, or gas mark 4). Start by coring the apples, and, if you're not using organic apples, peel them. Then cut the apples into similarly sized cubes. Place on a baking sheet and bake for about 10 minutes, or until they are very soft. Let cool, and mash them in a large bowl. Add the remaining ingredients and mix together thoroughly.

 Serving: Feed ¼ cup (50 g) twice a day to a medium-size cat; 1 cup (200 g) twice a day to a medium-size dog.

Green Turkey

This recipe is easy and nutritionally solid. You can substitute any boneless ground meat for the turkey and have a healthy meal for your pet.

3 pounds (1.5 kg) ground turkey meat,
preferably dark

1 egg

1 cup (120 g) finely chopped raw (or cooked and mashed) **seasonal produce** (any combination of carrots, zucchini, turnips, cabbage, beets, broccoli, cooked sweet potato, cooked winter squash, green beans, apples, berries, etc.)

¼ cup (7 g) finely chopped fresh dark, leafy greens (any combination of kale, spinach, lettuce, chard, parsley, escarole, chicory, dandelion, collards, etc.)

2 tablespoons (18 g) bonemeal

2 tablespoons (9 g) alfalfa powder

1 teaspoon granulated or **powdered garlic**

1 teaspoon kelp

1 teaspoon dulse

In a large bowl, mix all of the ingredients together thoroughly.

 Serving: Feed ¼ cup (50 g) twice a day to a medium-size cat; 1 cup (200 g) twice a day to a medium-size dog.

Sardines and Ground Turkey with Millet

4 cups (740 g) cooked millet (follow package directions)

3 pounds (1.5 kg) ground turkey meat, preferably dark

2 cans (3.5 ounces, or 100 g each) sardines

1 cup (120 g) finely chopped raw (or cooked and mashed) **seasonal produce** (any combination of carrots, zucchini, turnips, cabbage, beets, broccoli, cooked sweet potato, cooked winter squash, green beans, apples, berries, etc.)

2 tablespoons (18 g) bonemeal

2 tablespoons (9 g) alfalfa powder

You can use any poultry here instead of turkey. However, always keep variety in mind. Take time to think about the meat sources you usually use and make an effort to mix it up. I use my calendar as a log to note what main meat source I use each day.

In a large bowl, mix all of the ingredients together thoroughly.

 Serving: Feed about ⅓ cup (67 g) twice a day to a medium-size cat; 1½ cups (300 g) twice a day to a medium-size dog.

Oatmeal and Organ Meats

Polenta and Ground Lamb with Cruciferous Vegetables

Serving oatmeal is a nice way to feed your pet grains. This is another simple and elegant

2 cups (160 g) cooked oats (preferably The Ultimate Veggie Oats on page 102, but can be plain)

1 pound (455 g) ground organ meats, any combination

1 egg

1 teaspoon kelp

1 teaspoon dulse

1 teaspoon alfalfa powder

Let the oats cool, then thoroughly mix in the remaining ingredients.

 Serving: Feed about ⅓ cup (67 g) twice a day to a medium-size cat; 1½ cups (300 g) twice a day to a medium-size dog.

I tend to cook cruciferous vegetables such as broccoli, cauliflower, cabbage, Brussels sprouts, etc., when using them in my pet food recipes. The phytonutrients in them are a bit more available when cooked. Lamb is a great meat to use in your pet food, and although harder to find than beef, it is worth the effort to provide your pet with alternative nutrients.

2 cups (314 g) cooked polenta (follow package directions)

1 pound (455 g) ground lamb

½ cup (35 g) cooked chopped cruciferous vegetables

1 tablespoon (9 g) bonemeal

1 teaspoon alfalfa powder

In a large bowl, mix all of the ingredients together thoroughly.

 Serving: Feed about ⅓ cup (67 g) twice a day to a medium-size cat; 1½ cups (300 g) twice a day to a medium-size dog.

Barley and Jack Mackerel

Barley seems like a forgotten grain, but it is truly wonderful. It has a consistency that cats and dogs tend to enjoy and mixes well with any meats and veggies.

3 cups (471 g) cooked barley (follow package directions)

2 cans (14.75 ounces, or **418 g each) jack mackerel**

½ pound (227 g) ground organ meat

2 tablespoons (9 g) alfalfa powder

1 teaspoon kelp

1 teaspoon dulse

1 teaspoon granulated or **powdered garlic**

In a large bowl, mix all of the ingredients together thoroughly.

 Serving: Feed about ⅓ cup (67 g) twice a day to a medium-size cat; 1½ cups (300 g) twice a day to a medium-size dog.

Barley and Ground Turkey

This is another nutritionally solid, barley-inspired recipe.

4 cups (628 g) cooked barley (follow package directions)

2 pounds (910 g) ground turkey meat, preferably dark

1 egg

½ pound (227 g) ground organ meat

2 tablespoons (18 g) bonemeal

2 tablespoons (9 g) alfalfa powder

1 teaspoon kelp

1 teaspoon dulse

In a large bowl, mix all of the ingredients together thoroughly.

 Serving: Feed about ⅓ cup (67 g) twice a day to a medium-size cat; 1½ cups (300 g) twice a day to a medium-size dog.

Cooked Chicken Livers with Sardines

Scrambled Eggs with Salmon and Apple

This is a good recipe to use as you transition your cat or dog from a commercial diet to a homemade one. Although raw liver is healthier than cooked for your pet, many pets find raw livers difficult to accept. Cooking them lightly will make them smell great, and the addition of sardines makes this meal particularly tasty!

1 tablespoon (15 ml) olive oil

1 pound (455 g) chicken livers

3 cans (3.5 ounces, or 100 g each) sardines

Heat the olive oil in a skillet. Add the livers and cook for about 15 minutes, or until the outsides are firm. (I usually leave the interiors a little rare.) Let cool, then chop into bite-size pieces. Mix the livers with the sardines and serve.

 Serving: Feed ¼ cup (50 g) twice a day to a medium-size cat; 1 cup (200 g) twice a day to a medium-size dog.

 Variations: Cook ½ pound (227 g) of the livers; chop up the remaining ½ pound (227 g) of raw livers and stir them in with the sardines. You can also substitute ½ pound (227 g) of chopped raw chicken hearts for the livers.

This recipe also makes a great topping for The Ultimate Veggie Oats (see page 102) or other cooked grains.

This is a sweet food that many pets consider a treat.

1 dozen eggs

1 apple, diced

2 tablespoons (30 ml) olive oil

2 cans (14.75 ounces, or 418 g each) wild pink Alaskan salmon

In a large bowl, beat the eggs well. Add the apple and mix gently. Heat the olive oil in a large pan over medium-low heat and add the egg mixture, stirring as it cooks for scrambled eggs. Remove the pan from the heat and stir in the salmon.

 Serving: Feed ¼ cup (50 g) twice a day to a medium-size cat; 1 cup (200 g) twice a day to a medium-size dog.

 Variations: Use diced carrots instead of apple. You can also substitute sardines, jack mackerel, or ground chicken meat for the salmon.

Soft-Boiled Eggs, Steamed Spinach, and Salmon

Soft-boiled eggs are a good alternative to scrambled—my pets seem to really like the chunkiness.

Steam the spinach by putting about 1 tablespoon of water in a small saucepan, adding the spinach, and covering. It should be bright green and wilted within 5 minutes. Meanwhile, peel and chop the eggs. Put the steamed spinach into a bowl, add the eggs and salmon, and mix well.

 Serving: Feed ¼ cup (50 g) twice a day to a medium-size cat; 1 cup (200 g) twice a day to a medium-size dog.

 Variations: Substitute 1 pound (455 g) of raw ground chicken necks for the canned salmon.

1 cup (30 g) coarsely chopped spinach leaves

3 soft-boiled eggs

1 can (14.75 ounces, or 418 g) wild pink Alaskan salmon

Big Baked Veggies and Sautéed Chicken Thighs

2 beets

1 sweet potato

1 small butternut squash

3 tablespoons (45 ml) olive oil

3 tablespoons (7 g) minced fresh herbs or **2 tablespoons (4 g) dried mixed herbs** (rosemary, thyme, mint, sage, oregano, and/or marjoram, etc.)

2 pounds (910 g) boneless chicken thighs

1 clove garlic, minced

1 can (3.5 ounces, or 100 g) sardines

If you take out the sardines, this makes a tasty human meal as well!

Preheat oven to 350°F (180°C, or gas mark 4). Wash, peel, and cut up the beets, sweet potato, and squash into similarly sized pieces, about 1 inch. Place in a small oiled or buttered baking dish, and toss with about 1 tablespoon (15 ml) of the oil. Bake for 20 to 25 minutes, or until soft and lightly browned. Let cool, mash up, and mix in the herbs.

Rinse the chicken thighs and cut into strips. Heat the remaining olive oil in a skillet over medium heat. Add the chicken and garlic, and cook until the chicken is no longer pink inside, about 7 to 10 minutes. Remove from the heat and let cool. In a large bowl, mix the chicken, sardines, and vegetables together.

 Serving: Feed ¼ cup (50 g) twice a day to a medium-size cat; 1 cup (200 g) twice a day to a medium-size dog.

 Variations: If you aren't serving this as a human meal, you can leave the chicken on the rare side.

Yogurt or Soft Cheese Meal

Some pets do very well with dairy in their diets, but others don't. If you see a correlation between feeding dairy and some sort of allergy or digestive issue, stop feeding dairy—it's not necessary to your pet's diet. The yogurt in this recipe has great probiotic activity.

1 cup (230 g) plain yogurt or soft cheese

1 can (14.75 ounces, or 418 g) wild pink Alaskan salmon

½ cup (47 g) ground walnuts

½ cup (112 g) finely chopped raw zucchini, yellow squash, or other summer squash

In a large bowl, mix all of the ingredients together thoroughly.

 Serving: Feed ¼ cup (50 g) twice a day to a medium-size cat; 1 cup (200 g) twice a day to a medium-size dog.

Baby Shrimp and Carrots

Although slightly decadent, a shrimp-based meal is a great way to provide some extra diversity in your pet's meal plans.

2 tablespoons (30 ml, or 28 g) olive oil or butter

4 raw carrots, coarsely chopped

¼ cup (56 g) chopped chicken hearts

2 cans (4 ounces or 100 g each) wild pink baby shrimp (I use Wild Planet sustainably caught shrimp)

1 egg

2 tablespoons (18 g) alfalfa powder

Heat the olive oil or butter in a large skillet over medium-low heat. Add the carrots and sauté until soft. Add the chopped hearts and lightly cook. Drain the baby shrimp and place in a large bowl. Let the carrots and hearts cool down, then add them to the shrimp. Add the egg and alfalfa powder and mix thoroughly, mashing the carrots with a fork as you do so.

 Serving: Feed ¼ cup (50 g) twice a day to a medium-size cat; 1 cup (200 g) twice a day to a medium-size dog.

 Variations: Use canned clams instead of shrimp. Some cats and dogs love them, and they are a very healthy, balanced whole-food source.

Lamb and Salmon Patties with Wild Greens

My pets enjoy these patties both cooked and raw. You will probably find that your pet does too.

In a large bowl, mash up the lamb, salmon, egg, and greens until well mixed and moist enough to hold together to form patties. Add a little stock or water if the mixture is too dry. For a cat or small dog, form patties a little less than ½-inch (1.25 cm) thick and about 2 inches (5 cm) in diameter. For larger dogs, make hamburger-size patties.

Heat the olive oil in a skillet over medium heat. Put the patties in the pan; they should sizzle. Cook for about 2 minutes on each side for small patties and 4 minutes on each side for hamburger-size patties. They will still be rare in the center, and smell very tasty.

 Serving: Feed 1 or 2 small patties twice a day to a medium-size cat or small dog; 1 large patty twice a day to a medium-size dog.

Note: *There are two big rules to harvesting wild greens: Know exactly what you are harvesting, and harvest from safe areas, away from roads or yards or fields that may have been sprayed with pesticides or herbicides.*

 Variations: You can add ¼ cup (24 g) ground walnuts to this recipe.

2 cups (910 g) ground lamb meat

1 can (14.75 ounces, or 418 g) wild pink Alaskan salmon

1 egg

½ cup (15 g) minced wild fresh greens (dandelion, plantain, chickweed, lamb's quarters, sorrel, or other dark, leafy greens)

Chicken stock or water

2 tablespoons (30 ml) olive oil

Soft-Boiled Eggs, Barley, and Salmon

Oatmeal and Fish

Barley is another favorite grain that I like to use in my home-made pet food.

1 cup (157 g) cooked barley (follow package directions)

1 can (14.75 ounces, or 418 g) wild pink Alaskan salmon

3 soft-boiled eggs

1 teaspoon kelp

1 teaspoon dulse

1 teaspoon alfalfa powder

In a large bowl, mix all of the ingredients together thoroughly.

 Serving: Feed about ⅓ cup (67 g) twice a day to a medium-size cat; 1½ cups (300 g) twice a day to a medium-size dog.

For cats especially, you may find that the amounts of oats in this recipe are a bit too much. I suggest you cut back on the amount of oats if you are feeding a cat.

2 cups cooked (160 g) oats to feed a dog; **½ cup (40 g)** to feed a cat (preferably The Ultimate Veggie Oats on page 102, but can be plain)

1 can (14.75 ounces, or 418 g) jack mackerel or **wild pink Alaskan salmon**

1 can (3.5 ounces, or 100 g) sardines

1 egg

1 teaspoon kelp

1 teaspoon dulse

1 teaspoon alfalfa powder

Let the oats cool, then thoroughly mix in the remaining ingredients.

 Serving: Feed about ⅓ cup (67 g) twice a day to a medium-size cat; 1½ cups (300 g) twice a day to a medium-size dog.

Chicken Breasts with Cauliflower and Parsnips

This recipe makes a very civilized gourmet meal for your pets.

In a large pot, combine the garlic, cauliflower, parsnips, and broth and bring to a boil. Simmer for about ½ hour, or until the vegetables are tender.

Meanwhile, rinse the chicken breasts and cut into strips. Heat 2 tablespoons (30 ml) of the olive oil over medium heat in a skillet. Add the chicken and oregano and cook, stirring occasionally, until cooked through, about 7 to 10 minutes.

Add the chicken to the broth mixture and stir in 1 cup (165 g) of the rice or barley for a chunky, porridge-like consistency. Add more rice or barley if it is too soupy. Add the remaining ¼ cup (60 ml) olive oil, mix well, and let cool before serving.

 Serving: Feed about ⅓ cup (67 g) twice a day to a medium-size cat; 1½ cups (300 g) twice a day to a medium-size dog.

 Variations: You can leave the chicken raw, cube it, and add it to the cooled vegetables and grains. You can also sprinkle on a little kelp and dulse or some Herb and Spice Healthy Supplement Powder (see page 69) when serving.

1 clove garlic, roughly chopped

2 cups (200 g) chopped cauliflower, cut into ½-inch pieces

2 cups (450 g) chopped parsnips, cut into ½-inch pieces

5 cups (1.2 L) chicken or beef broth

2 pounds (910 g) boneless chicken breasts, with skins

2 tablespoons (30 ml) plus ¼ cup (60 ml) olive oil

1 teaspoon dried oregano

1 to 2 cups (165 to 330 g) cooked rice or barley (follow package directions)

Polenta and Sardines with Zucchini

I really love mixing up this recipe, especially in midsummer when fresh zucchini and other summer squash are readily available in grocery stores and farmers' markets.

2 cups (314 g) cooked polenta (follow package directions)

2 cans (3.5 ounces, or 100 g each) sardines

1 cup (225 g) minced raw (or cooked and mashed) **summer squash** or **zucchini**

1 tablespoon (4.5 g) alfalfa powder

1 can (14.75 ounces, or 418 g) jack mackerel or **wild pink Alaskan salmon**

In a large bowl, mix all of the ingredients together thoroughly.

 Serving: Feed about ⅓ cup (67 g) twice a day to a medium-size cat; 1½ cups (300 g) twice a day to a medium-size dog.

Polenta, Jack Mackerel, and Scrambled Eggs

Here's another great summer squash recipe, although the squash can easily be replaced by another vegetable. The last time I made this, I used ¼ cup (7 g) of raw minced kale and spinach.

4 eggs

1 tablespoon (15 ml) olive oil

2 cups (314 g) cooked polenta (follow package directions)

1 can (14.75 ounces, or 418 g) jack mackerel

½ cup (65 g) cooked mashed carrots

1 cup (225 g) minced raw (or cooked and mashed) **summer squash** or **zucchini**

1 tablespoon (4.5 g) alfalfa powder

In a large bowl, beat the eggs well. Heat the olive oil in a medium pan over medium-low heat and add the beaten eggs, stirring as they cook for scrambled-style eggs. Remove the pan from the heat and let cool. Transfer to a large bowl, add all of the remaining ingredients, and mix together thoroughly.

 Serving: Feed about ⅓ cup (67 g) twice a day to a medium-size cat; 1½ cups (300 g) twice a day to a medium-size dog.

 Variations: To save time, use canned organic carrots instead of steaming or baking fresh ones.

Canned Fish Trio and Baked Winter Squash with Millet

Nettle Rice

Millet is a nice mild grain, which I find most pets like more than quinoa, which can be a tad bitter or off-putting.

Here's a light-protein meal, good for providing variation. This also works well as an occasional fasting meal.

1 small butternut, acorn, delicata, kuri, or other winter squash

1 can (14.75 ounces, or 418 g) wild pink Alaskan salmon

1 can (14.75 ounces, or 418 g) jack mackerel

2 cans (3.5 ounces, or 100 g each) sardines

1 egg

¼ cup (7 g) finely chopped fresh dark, leafy greens (any combination of kale, spinach, lettuce, chard, parsley, escarole, chicory, dandelion, collards, etc.)

3 cups (555 g) cooked millet (follow package directions)

Short-grain brown rice

1 cup (28 g) dried stinging nettle

1 can (14.75 ounces, or 418 g) wild pink Alaskan salmon

1 can (3.5 ounces, or 100 g) sardines

1 egg

Preheat oven to 350°F (180°C, or gas mark 4). Cut the squash in half. Place the halves skin-side-up on a baking sheet and bake for 1 to 1½ hours (depending on the size of the squash), or until the skin starts to blister and caramelize.

Let the squash cool, then scoop out the flesh into a large bowl. Add the salmon, mackerel, sardines, egg, and chopped greens and mash with the squash. Mix in the millet.

Following the package directions, make 4 cups (660 g) of cooked rice for a dog or 2 cups (330 g) of cooked rice for a cat. When the rice is almost finished cooking, and still has some excess moisture in it, mix in the stinging nettle. Continue cooking until the rice is done. Remove from the heat and let cool, then mix in the salmon, sardines, and egg.

 Serving: Feed about ⅓ cup (67 g) twice a day to a medium-size cat; 1½ cups (300 g) twice a day to a medium-size dog.

 Serving: Feed about ⅓ cup (67 g) twice a day to a medium-size cat; 1½ cups (300 g) twice a day to a medium-size dog.

Note: *Stinging nettle is a chlorophyll-rich and mineral-rich green food. If you cannot find stinging nettle, you can substitute dried parsley, which is another mineral-rich green food.*

 Variations: Substitute barley for the brown rice.

Oatmeal and Eggs

This is a simple and elegant, quick meal. Feel free to vary the amounts of either the oats or eggs to provide variety.

While the oats are still hot, add the eggs and stir thoroughly (this slightly cooks the eggs). Serve this meal warm or at room temperature. Instead of plain oats, the photo (opposite) shows Veggie Oats from page 102.

 Serving: Feed about ⅓ cup (67 g) twice a day to a medium-size cat; 1½ cups (300 g) twice a day to a medium-size dog.

 Variations: I usually sprinkle some dried oregano, stinging nettle, and kelp/dulse into the oats to give them a savory flavor.

2 cups (160 g) cooked oats (preferably The Ultimate Veggie Oats on page 102, but can be plain)

4 eggs

Zucchini and Eggs

1 dozen eggs

2 small/medium zucchini (or any summer squash), cut into ½-inch (1.25 cm) cubes

3 tablespoons (45 ml) olive oil

This is a great recipe that can be made in any quantity. Best of all, this dish is a delicious breakfast for your family as well as your pets.

Beat the eggs well in a large bowl. Add the zucchini cubes and salt and pepper and mix thoroughly. Heat the olive oil in a large pan over medium-low heat. Add the egg mixture, stirring as it cooks for scrambled-style eggs. Sprinkle with salt and pepper to taste if serving humans.

 Serving: Feed about ⅓ cup (67 g) twice a day to a medium-size cat; 1½ cups (300 g) twice a day to a medium-size dog.

 Variations: Substitute fresh asparagus, trimmed and cut into ½-inch (1.25 cm) pieces, for the zucchini.

Scrambled Eggs with Broccoli

1 dozen eggs

2 cups (140 g) fresh broccoli florets, steamed (or 1 package [9 ounces, or 255 g] frozen broccoli florets, cooked according to package directions)

3 tablespoons (45 ml) olive oil

Salt, to taste

Pepper, to taste

I've found that most dogs and many cats love steamed broccoli florets. But if your family members aren't fans, you can make this with their favorite vegetables instead of the broccoli—your pets won't mind!

Beat the eggs well in a large bowl. Add the broccoli and mix together gently. Heat the olive oil in a large pan over medium-low heat and add the egg mixture, stirring as it cooks for scrambled eggs. Add the salt and pepper to taste.

 Serving: Feed about ⅓ cup (67 g) twice a day to a medium-size cat; 1½ cups (300 g) twice a day to a medium-size dog.

 Variations:
- Add a can of sardines to the beaten eggs along with the other ingredients, for a dose of extra nutrients.
- You can substitute cauliflower, Brussels sprouts, or other vegetables for the broccoli florets.

Beef Strips Stir-Fry

A variation on the Chicken Thigh Stir-Fry (see page 152), this is another one-pot, after-work healthy meal for all to enjoy.

Rinse the beef strips and pat excess water away with a paper towel. Heat the olive oil in a large skillet over medium heat. Add beef, garlic, oregano, and vegetables. Cook, stirring, for about 5 minutes, or until the beef is desired doneness. Add garlic granules, salt, and pepper.

 Serving: Feed ¼ cup (50 g) twice a day to a medium-size cat; 1 cup (200 g) twice a day to a medium-size dog.

 Variations: To add more bulk, serve the stir-fry over brown rice. When serving this stir-fry to my animals, I usually sprinkle a little kelp and dulse or some Herb and Spice Healthy Supplement Powder (see page 69) over it.

2 pounds (910 g) pepper steak–style beef strips (or cut strips from a larger piece of beef)

3 tablespoons (45 ml) olive oil

1 clove garlic, minced

1 teaspoon dried oregano

1 cup (120 g) vegetables and greens (any combination of zucchini, broccoli, kale, spinach, diced turnips, bok choy, etc.)

1 teaspoon garlic granules or **powder**

Salt, to taste

Pepper, to taste

Chicken Thigh Stir-Fry

2 pounds (910 g) boneless chicken thighs

3 tablespoons (45 ml) olive oil

1 clove garlic, minced

1 teaspoon dried oregano

1 cup (120 g) vegetables and greens (any combination of zucchini, broccoli, kale, spinach, diced turnips, bok choy, etc.)

1 teaspoon garlic granules or powder

Salt, to taste

Pepper, to taste

This is a quick and easy one-pot meal the whole household will enjoy.

Rinse the chicken thighs and cut into strips. Heat the olive oil in a large skillet over medium heat. Add chicken, garlic, oregano, and vegetables. Cook, stirring, for about 5 minutes, or until the chicken is cooked through. Remove from the heat and add the garlic granules, salt, and pepper.

 Serving: Feed ¼ cup (50 g) twice a day to a medium-size cat; 1 cup (200 g) twice a day to a medium-size dog.

 Variations:
- To add more bulk, serve the stir-fry over brown rice.
- When serving this stir-fry to my animals, I usually sprinkle a little kelp and dulse or some Herb and Spice Healthy Supplement Powder (see page 69) over it.

Sardine Salad

1 can (3.5 ounces, or 100 g) whole sardines in olive oil (not skinless, boneless)

3 tablespoons (48 g) cocktail sauce

This is really delicious; I enjoy the fact that I can lick the fork that I use to serve this food to my cats!

Scoop the sardines out of the can and onto a plate; discard the extra oil. With a fork, mash the sardines into a smooth consistency. Add the cocktail sauce and mix thoroughly.

 Serving: Provides 2 meals for most cats; 1 meal for most dogs.

 Variations:

- Healthy additions to this recipe are 1 to 2 tablespoons (14 to 28 g) of cooked peas or 1 to 2 tablespoons (15 to 30 g) of plain yogurt.
- You can also vary the flavor and consistency by making your own cocktail sauce. Cocktail sauce is just ketchup with horseradish added. You can use premade, but avoid any brands with high-fructose corn syrup. You can make your own in one of two ways: Use organic ketchup and simply grate fresh horseradish root into it to taste; or use canned tomato paste, adding a dash of apple cider vinegar, a sprinkle of sugar, a dash of salt, and a grating of horseradish root. Keep tasting and adding little bits of horseradish until you like the flavor.
- You can buy prepared horseradish, but chunks of fresh root are usually available in most grocery stores. Simply wash and peel part of the root, and grate on a fine cheese grater. Wrap and freeze the unused portion; it lasts several months in the freezer and is actually easier to grate once frozen.

Turkey and Veggie Frittata

2 cups (140 g) cut-up cruciferous **vegetables** (broccoli, cauliflower, and/or Brussels sprouts) in even-size pieces

4 or **5 eggs**

2 cups (280 g) cooked turkey **meat** (about 10 ounces), cut into bite-size pieces

1 teaspoon paprika

1 teaspoon turmeric

1 tablespoon (15 ml) olive oil

Frittatas are easy to make, quick to serve, and store well in the refrigerator. Add some salt and pepper (to taste) if you are eating this along with your pets.

Bring about 3 cups (705 ml) of water to a boil in a medium saucepan. Add the vegetables and simmer for 10 minutes, or until fork-tender. Remove from the heat and drain.

Beat the eggs in a large bowl; add turkey, vegetables, paprika, and turmeric. Mix well.

Warm the olive oil in a large skillet over low heat, coating the bottom of the skillet lightly with the oil. Once the oil is hot, pour in the egg mixture. Cover and cook over very low heat until the center is relatively solid, about 20 to 30 minutes. Slice into 8 pieces and serve.

 Serving: Feed 1 slice (⅛ of frittata) to a medium-size cat; 2 slices to a medium- or large-size dog.

 Variations: You can substitute chicken for the turkey and cut-up summer vegetables such as zucchini, yellow squash, and asparagus for the cruciferous vegetables.

Turkey, Pea, and Sote Potato Frittata

This frittata comes out more puffy and starchy than the Turkey and Veggie Frittata on page 156.

Beat the eggs in a large bowl. Add the turkey, peas, sweet potato, paprika, turmeric, and cumin. Mix well.

Warm the olive oil in a large skillet over low heat, coating the bottom of the skillet lightly with the oil. Once the oil is hot, pour in the egg mixture. Cover and cook over very low heat until the center is relatively solid, about 20 to 30 minutes. Slice into 8 pieces and serve.

 Serving: Feed 1 slice (⅛ of frittata) to a medium-size cat; 2 slices to a medium- or large-size dog.

Note: *Although turmeric is usually well liked by dogs and cats, cumin can be a bit strong for some, especially cats. If you wish, add some salt and pepper (to taste) if you are eating this along with your pets.*

 Variations:

- You can substitute chicken for the turkey.
- Although I don't feed many vegetables from the nightshade family to my pets, potatoes are mild and would work very nicely in this recipe, especially if you don't have sweet potatoes. Any variety of potato can be used, but never use potatoes that have started to turn green or have sprouts.

4 or 5 eggs

2 cups (280 g) cooked turkey meat (about 10 ounces), cut into bite-size pieces

½ **cup (65 g) frozen peas**

½ **cup chopped** or **grated sweet potato**

1 teaspoon paprika

1 teaspoon turmeric

Pinch of cumin

1 tablespoon (15 ml) olive oil

Meatloaf

4 **slices whole grain bread**, torn up

⅔ cup (156 ml) milk

2 **pounds (910 g) ground beef (85% lean)**

2 **eggs**, beaten

1 **teaspoon salt**

1 **clove garlic**, coarsely chopped

½ **teaspoon garlic powder**

3 **tablespoons (45 g) ketchup**

1 **tablespoon (15 ml) Worcestershire sauce**

Pepper, to taste

Here's my mom's recipe for family meatloaf, with just a few changes to make it healthier for cats and dogs.

Preheat oven to 350°F (180°C, or gas mark 4). In a small bowl, soak the bread in the milk. In a large bowl, mix the remaining ingredients together along with the bread and any leftover milk. Don't overwork, but make sure it is well mixed. Form into a log shape on a deep-edged baking sheet. Bake for about 1½ hours if the human members of the household will be sharing this meal. If it's just for your pets, bake just until the outside gets crusty and savory and the interior stays rare. Let cool, then serve to your pets.

 Serving: I usually slice this into 1-inch thick (2.5 cm thick) slices so each slice ends up being about a 4 x 6 x 1-inch (10 x 15 x 2.5 cm) rectangle. Feed ½ slice (67 g) twice a day to a medium-size cat; 1½ slices (300 g) twice a day to a medium-size dog.

Healthy Snacks and Treats

Treats are an important food for building relationships and can also be used as effective positive reinforcement tools. Some treats are very simple, whole foods that your pet likes. It is good to provide a variety of treats, but don't overdo it. Keep portions small, and remember that you want your pet to fully rest his or her digestive system between meals.

Here are some of my favorite whole-food treats, many of which are easy to distribute and carry.

- **Raw carrots**: These can be whole for a large dog, or cut into sticks for a smaller dog.

- **Cucumber or melon chunks**: Cats and dogs can both enjoy these refreshing raw treats.

- **Bonito flakes**: Cats usually love these fishy flakes.

- **Cheese**: Use small amounts at first to make sure your pet doesn't have issues digesting cheese.

- **Olives**: Serve them without pits, of course; dogs and many cats usually love olives.

- **Smelts**: These small fish can be fed either whole and raw or cooked lightly.

- **Alfalfa or mung bean sprouts**: I usually sprout these myself in a covered bowl. Simply buy alfalfa or mung sprouting seeds (make sure they are labeled for sprouting). Pour about ¼ cup (12 g) into a medium bowl and cover with water. Twice a day, rinse and freshen the water. After a couple of days, the seeds will sprout. Continue to rinse the sprouts two or three times a day, but strain them after rinsing and don't fill the bowl with water. Sprouts should be kept covered and at room temperature. They will last about one week on the kitchen counter after sprouting. As soon as the seeds start sprouting, they can be fed as treats or used in your meal plans. I find that some cats really enjoy them because the little sprouts have a certain movement to them that promotes some play.

- **Dehydrated liver pieces**: Cut beef liver into strips and dehydrate according to your dehydrator directions for jerky. Or if you don't have a dehydrator, you can place the liver strips in boiling water, cook completely, and drain. Spread the cooked strips on a baking sheet and place in a 200°F (90°C) oven for about 2 hours, or until they feel completely dry and lightweight.

- **Beef marrow or leg bones**: These are really more for dogs rather than cats. I use beef marrow bones or leg bones, cut into rounds 2- to 3- inches (5 to 7.5 cm) high and at least ½-inch (1.25 cm) thick all the way around. Try to purchase bones from grass-fed cows if at all possible because they tend to be thicker and stronger and less prone to splintering. I usually dip them in boiling water for about 2 minutes, just to clean off any surface bacteria, let them cool down thoroughly, and then pass them out to the dogs. They love gnawing on them.

  You do want to make sure the dogs stay on an easy-to-clean floor; this treat will need monitoring for safety as it makes a mess. It seems dogs always end up sneaking into rooms with rugs with the bones because the rug texture provides better leverage!

  Also, once you hand them to your dog, be present and watchful. You want to make sure your dog isn't getting big hunks off the bone or splintering or cracking the bone. Also monitor the marrow—make sure your dog can reach it with his or her tongue and not try to force his or her jaw into the center of the bone.

You can also cook up more elaborate treats and snacks. Most of the following treat recipes have meat in them, so it's best to store them in the refrigerator. They can also be frozen. I like to give frozen ones to teething pups.

Cornmeal-Chicken Muffins

2 eggs

⅓ **cup (78 ml) milk**

1 tablespoon (15 ml) coconut oil

1 tablespoon (20 g) honey

⅓ **cup (75 ml) puréed raw chicken hearts and liver**

1 cup (140 g) cornmeal

½ **cup (63 g) white flour**

Most treats tend to be crunchy, but these are softer and chewy. Of all the baked treats I make, my cats like these best.

Preheat oven to 350°F (180°C, or gas mark 4). Grease or line two standard or mini muffin pans with paper liners. (Use the standard size for medium and large dogs; the mini size for cats and small dogs.)

In a small bowl, mix the eggs, milk, oil, honey, and puréed organ meats and set aside. In a large bowl, mix the cornmeal and flour. Make a well in the center, and pour in the egg mixture. Mix thoroughly.

Pour the batter into the prepared muffin pans. Fill each cup about three-quarters full. You will have enough batter for about 12 to 15 standard-size muffins or about 30 mini muffins.

Bake for 15 to 20 minutes for standard-size muffins or 8 to 12 minutes for mini muffins), or until the muffins sound hard when tapped on the top. They won't rise a lot when baking, but they will harden and stay chewy after cooling. Store the muffins in the refrigerator.

 Serving: About 1 muffin snack per day as a treat.

Liver and Parsley Crescent Biscuits

If you are a fan of liver, you will really like how these smell as they bake.

Preheat oven to 375° F (190°C, or gas mark 5). In a small bowl, mix the molasses, honey, water, oil, parsley, and liver and set aside. In a large bowl, mix the flour and ground pumpkin seeds. Make a well in the center, and pour in the molasses mixture. Mix thoroughly; you'll probably have to work the dough with your hands, and depending on the moisture levels in the liver, you may need to add a bit more flour so the dough isn't too sticky to work with.

Shape the dough into flattened crescent shapes. You can make large crescents (about 2.5-inches [6.25 cm] wide), or smaller ones (about 1-inch [2.5 cm] wide). I usually split the dough in half and do half large for my dogs and half small for my cats. This recipe will make about 18 large crescents or 32 small crescents. Place on a baking sheet, and bake for 15 minutes for large crescents or 8 minutes for small ones, or until they start to brown a bit around the edges. They won't rise when baking, but will harden and stay chewy after cooling. Store the biscuits in the refrigerator.

 Serving: About 1 crescent snack per day as a treat.

1 tablespoon (20 g) molasses

1 tablespoon (20 g) honey

1¼ cups (295 ml) water

1 tablespoon (15 ml) olive oil

¼ cup (5 g) dried parsley

½ cup (113 g) chopped raw beef liver

2½ cups (313 g) whole wheat flour

½ cup (48 g) ground pumpkin seeds

Love Biscuits

1 tablespoon (20 g) molasses

1 tablespoon (20 g) honey

1¼ cups (295 ml) water

1 tablespoon (15 ml) olive oil

¼ cup dried (8 g) stinging nettle

½ cup (227 g) chopped raw
chicken hearts

3 cups (375) whole wheat flour

I love shaping these chewy chicken-heart biscuits into hearts!

Preheat oven to 375°F (190°C, or gas mark 5).

In a small bowl, mix molasses, honey, water, oil, stinging nettle, and chicken hearts and set aside. Place the flour in a large bowl, make a well in the center, and pour in the molasses mixture. Mix thoroughly; you'll probably have to work the dough with your hands, and depending on the moisture level in the hearts, you may need to add a bit more flour so the dough isn't too sticky to work with.

Shape the dough into flattened heart shapes. You can make large hearts (about 2.5-inches [6.25 cm] wide), or smaller ones (about 1.5-inches [3.75 cm] wide). I usually split the dough in half and do half large for my dogs and half small for my cats. This recipe will make about 18 large hearts or 32 small hearts. Place on a baking sheet and bake for 15 minutes for large hearts or 8 minutes for small ones, or until they start to brown a bit around the edges. They won't rise when baking, but will harden and stay chewy after cooling. Store the biscuits in the refrigerator.

 Serving: About 1 biscuit per day as a treat.

Figgy Biscuits

Dried figs and dates are so mineral- and nutrient-rich that these treats are truly healthy whole-food supplements for your pet—and the people in your household can eat them as well!

Preheat oven to 375°F (190°C, or gas mark 5). In a small bowl, mix the molasses, honey, water, oil, dried fruits, and walnuts and set aside. Place the flour and salt in a large bowl and mix well. Make a well in the center and pour in the molasses mixture. Mix thoroughly.

Shape the dough into flattened crescent shapes. You can make large crescents (about 2.5-inches [6.25 cm] wide), or smaller ones (about 1-inch [2.5 cm] wide). I usually split the dough in half and do half large for my dogs and half small for my cats. This recipe will make about 18 large crescents or 32 small crescents. Place on a baking sheet and bake for 15 minutes for large crescents or 8 minutes for small ones, or until they start to brown a bit around the edges. They won't rise when baking, but will harden and stay chewy after cooling.

 Serving: About 1 crescent snack per day as a treat.

1 tablespoon (20 g) molasses

1 tablespoon (20 g) honey

1⅓ cups (315 ml) water

2 tablespoons (30 ml) olive oil

½ cup chopped dried figs and/or dates

½ cup chopped walnuts

3 cups (375 g) whole wheat flour

1 teaspoon salt

Coconut and Turmeric Biscuits

1 tablespoon (20 g) molasses

1 tablespoon (20 g) honey

1⅓ (315 ml) cups water

2 tablespoons (30 ml) coconut oil

½ cup (43 g) desiccated coconut flakes (not sweetened)

3 cups (375 g) whole wheat flour

1 tablespoon (7 g) turmeric

These super-healthy biscuits are a big favorite with my dogs, and are quite enjoyable for humans as well!

Preheat oven to 375°F (190°C, or gas mark 5). In a small bowl, mix the molasses, honey, water, oil, and coconut and set aside. In a large bowl, mix the flour and turmeric, make a well in the center, and pour in the molasses mixture. Mix thoroughly.

Shape the dough into flattened crescent shapes. You can make large crescents (about 2.5-inches [6.25 cm] wide), or smaller ones (about 1-inch [2.5 cm] wide). I usually split the dough in half and do half large for my dogs and half small for my cats. This recipe will make about 18 large crescents or 32 small crescents. Place on a baking sheet and bake for 15 minutes for large crescents or 8 minutes for small ones, or until they start to brown a bit around the edges. They won't rise when baking, but will harden and stay chewy after cooling.

 Serving: About 1 crescent snack per day as a treat.

Dill and Dulse Crackers

Although cats don't usually find these too exciting (unless you substitute bonito flakes for the dill), humans and dogs both really love them.

1 teaspoon dill seeds

2 tablespoons (28 g) butter

½ cup (63 g) flour

Pinch of salt

1 teaspoon dulse flakes

Dash of pepper

Preheat oven to 400°F (200°C, or gas mark 6). Crush the dill seeds, but not into powder, in a mortar and pestle or with a quick pulse in a food processor.

In a medium bowl, combine the butter, flour, salt, dulse flakes, pepper, and dill seeds. Mix well. On a lightly oiled baking sheet, divide the dough into 12 equal portions. Roll into balls. Position the 12 balls on the baking sheet and flatten each with the bottom of a glass to about ¼-inch thick. Bake for 7 to 10 minutes, or until just lightly browned.

 Serving: One whole cracker for larger dogs as a treat once or twice a day, or break a cracker into smaller pieces for training or for smaller dogs and cats.

Appendix 1

Foods That Are Particularly High in Specific Nutrients

This list is a generalized highlighting of the important characteristics of some of my favorite ingredients used in making healthy cat and dog food. Note that these are not the only nutrients in these foods; they are just the most prevalent ones.

Alfalfa Not only is it one of the most protein-rich green foods, but alfalfa also contains a wide range of nutrients and minerals, including vitamin A, amino acids, B-complex, biotin, vitamin C, calcium, chromium, copper, vitamin D, vitamin E, folate, iodine, iron, vitamin K, magnesium, manganese, phosphorus, potassium, selenium, silicon, sodium, trace minerals, and zinc. It's one of the most nutritionally rich foods.

Almonds A strengthening food, almonds contain calcium, magnesium, phosphorus, potassium, trace minerals, healthy fat, and protein.

Apples The nutrients and fiber in apples are effective for building beneficial bacteria in the digestive tract, promoting general intestinal health, and detoxifying.

Beets The dark color assures us of a high antioxidant level, and beets also contain good amounts of vitamin C, folate, and potassium. They are detoxifying and known for promoting general digestive system health.

Berries Berries top the charts in antioxidant levels; they are high in vitamin C, folate, and manganese (particularly raspberries). All berries are considered to be general tonics and detoxifiers, and blueberries and bilberries are proven promoters of eye health.

Brazil nuts As with most nuts, they contain healthy fat and protein. Brazil nuts also have a wide range of minerals and nutrients, including calcium, vitamin E, magnesium, phosphorus, potassium, high amounts of selenium, trace minerals, and zinc.

Broccoli, **cauliflower**, and **cabbage** These cruciferous vegetables possess high levels of antioxidants and are known for their cancer-suppressing abilities. They also promote general good health and healing.

Carob Carob is noted for promoting digestive tract health, as well as for its high levels of trace minerals and calcium.

Carrots The orange color assures high beta-carotene levels and eye-supporting nutrients. Carrots are also amazing healers, hormone balancers, and detoxifiers. In addition, they promote healthy skin and digestive systems.

Fennel bulb, **fennel seed**, and **anise seed** Soothing and healing for the stomach and digestive tract, these licorice-flavored ingredients are also full of trace minerals and aid in detoxification.

Figs Figs are full of nutrients and energy; they are restorative and energizing.

Garlic One of the oldest medicinals, garlic is known for healing and supporting all aspects of the body. It is an antibacterial, detoxifier, vermifuge, and antifungal, among many other things.

Honey Honey is an energizing food. Full of nutrients in forms that can be found in no other food, it also promotes healing.

Kale and **collards** These dark, leafy greens are known for their cancer-suppressing and detoxifying abilities; they are rich in antioxidants, vitamin C, calcium, and trace minerals.

Kelp and **dulse** Very nutritionally dense foods, kelp and dulse contain many of the most necessary nutrients and are solid sources of iodine. They also contain vitamin A, B-complex, biotin, vitamin C, calcium, choline, chromium, copper, vitamin E, inositol, iodine, iron, vitamin K, magnesium, manganese, phosphorus, potassium, selenium, silicon, sodium, trace minerals, and zinc.

Oregano A powerful herb, oregano strengthens the digestive tract and urinary tract, as well as supports general immunity and health.

Parsley and **stinging nettle** These herbs are super greens and restore and heal on the cellular level. They are also high in minerals and trace minerals, and are perfect detoxifiers for the digestive and urinary systems.

Pumpkin seeds (pepitas) Pumpkin seeds are good sources of healthy fat and protein and are high in minerals including magnesium, potassium, trace minerals, and zinc. They have been connected with increased muscle health and are also a proven vermifuge.

Sesame seeds (tahini) These tiny seeds need to be crushed or ground for optimal metabolizing of the powerful nutrients they contain: calcium, vitamin E, magnesium, phosphorus, potassium, trace minerals, and zinc, as well as healthy fat and protein.

Spinach and **Swiss chard** High in folate, potassium, and trace minerals, these dark, leafy greens are particularly good at detoxifying the digestive tract and supporting well-being in the body in general.

Sunflower seeds Nourishing on the cellular level, these protein-packed seeds also contain B-complex, vitamin D, vitamin E, folate, selenium, and a plethora of trace minerals.

Sweet potatoes An energizing and very complete food, sweet potatoes contain a full gamut of antioxidants, minerals, and vitamins.

Turmeric A super spice, turmeric is full of the powerful antioxidant curcumin, among others. It is credited with great powers of detoxification, healing of the liver and digestive system, and as a powerful anti-inflammatory.

Walnuts Rich in good fat and protein, walnuts are also good sources of B-complex, vitamin E, and a full array of the important minerals and trace minerals.

Appendix 2

Some Favorite High-Quality Commercial Food Brands (If You Cannot Make Your Own Pet Food)

Although it would be hard to find a commercially made food product that would be as good as what you can make at home, there are quite a few great options available by companies with good intentions. Here's a rundown of some super-high-quality commercial food products that are now available.

Canned

There are many solid options available; look for one where a specifically named meat (for example, lamb or beef heart) is the first ingredient, which means that the food has more of that ingredient weight-wise than any other. Avoid any with generalized terms such as meat or poultry by-products. The food should have limited amounts of grain or vegetable by-products; in other words, things such as wheat bran and potato starch should be listed low in the ingredient list. Whole vegetables and grains should be higher in the ingredient list, but a specific meat should always be first.

Some of the brands of canned food that currently appeal to me are Candidae/Felidae, Natural Balance, Orijen, Gro, Wellness, Merrick, Blue Buffalo, Evanger's, Nature's Variety (Prairie and Instinct), and Natura (a full line of great brands including Innova and EVO).

As with homemade pet food, variety is key here, too: Mix and match the brands and flavors. Don't just feed one type. Finally, this list is not exhaustive in any way; there are many other great super-quality canned foods available.

Kibble or Dry Food

Kibble is as easy and convenient as it gets time-wise, and sometimes I am happy to have a nice fresh bag available on a very busy evening. However, it is the least healthy way to feed your pet. Kibble goes bad fast; be sure to check the expiration date on the bag and buy from a source that gets a lot of traffic. If the bag is dusty, don't buy it! As with canned foods, you want to see specific meats named at the top of the ingredients list, such as turkey or chicken liver.

Some of the brands of dry food that currently appeal to me are Candidae/Felidae, Lotus, Natural Balance, Blue Buffalo, PetGuard, Nature's Variety (Prairie and Instinct), and Natura (a full line of great brands including Innova and EVO).

Don't forget that variety is key; mix and match the brands and flavors. And as above, this list is not exhaustive in any way; there are many other great super-quality kibbles available.

Frozen

If I couldn't make my own pet food, I would use frozen commercial foods; they are made up of raw meat and usually even have ground bone. Be aware that some are fully balanced meals and some are just the meat portion, requiring you to appropriately add your own ingredients to the food. Read the labels carefully and follow the directions. Here is a list of some of my favorites that closely mimic what you would be making yourself with a meat grinder in your kitchen: Nature's Variety, BRAVO, Darwin's Natural, Stella and Chewy's, Steve's Real Food for Pets, Primal Pet Foods, and Fresh Is Best.

Again, be sure to mix and match the brands and flavors to provide your pet with a variety of nutrients. And this list is not exhaustive in any way; there are many other high-quality frozen pet foods available.

Acknowledgments

First and foremost, I must acknowledge my great gratitude to all the wonderful cats and dogs that have been a part of my life as teachers and as inspiration for the writing of this book.

I also must thank my husband, Mark, and my sister, Suzanne, for all their constant support and encouragement.

Growing up, my parents filled my sister's and my own childhoods with pets and with connections to nature and gardening. My mother always thought for herself and made the health decisions for our family based on common sense and her own research, much of which was considered "alternative." I was brought up thinking "outside the box" and seeing holistic and integrative thinking as both normal and expected. To our family, eating natural, whole, home-cooked food was routine and thoroughly enjoyed. Organic food was an imperative, and my father has maintained an organic garden that provides our family with vegetables every single year. So I must strongly thank my parents for that powerful foundation that directly led to me being able to develop my feeding program for my animals and to write this book.

I must thank Aurora, our Alaskan Malamute who first started us on the journey of developing a homemade feeding program. And I also want to thank Dr. Kenneth Fischer, who was Aurora's veterinarian back in 1996 and who actively supported and encouraged my homemade meals, and provided much-appreciated guidance. Dr. Fischer is the owner of Hillsdale Animal Hospital, an integrative veterinary practice in Hillsdale, NJ. He blends the worlds of alternative/complementary care (clinical nutrition, acupuncture, chiropractic, herbal medicine, homeopathy, and bioenergetic medicine) and conventional medicine, surgery, and dentistry. Dr. Fischer feels strongly that the proper care of any pet begins with holistic nutrition.

One of the biggest forces propelling me to write this book are the people I have taught in workshops or have worked with as health-coaching clients along with their animals and their stories. It is that broad web of their stories and health histories that provided me with the experiences and inspiration to start really compiling and organizing my program.

I also was very strongly influenced and inspired by the writings of Juliette de Baïracli Levy, Richard H. Pitcairn, and Kymythy R. Schultze. Their books will have a prime spot on my bookshelves forever. *Whole Dog Journal*, a wonderful magazine on all aspects of raising dogs using holistic health and positive training and relationship building, is another influence and reference I would not have been the same without.

The influences of human-focused health experts and the Institute for Integrative Nutrition also played a very big role in the approach I take to pet health. I also want to thank Samantha Storey at the *New York Times* for her great article on home cooking for cats and dogs in 2011.

Finally, I must thank Jill Alexander at Fair Winds for her initial vision of this book and for her thoughtful and creative direction. Jennifer Bright Reich, Amy Kovalski, Cheryl Winters-Tetreau, Linda Hager, and Nanette Bendyna have also put tremendous thoughtfulness and work into this project, and this truly is a better book because of their efforts.

About the Author

Barbara Taylor-Laino has been developing recipes and making and feeding homemade food to her pets since 1996. She is a certified holistic health coach for humans, has extensively studied and researched feline and canine nutrition, and has integrated the two fields of study into an effective program for vibrant health for cats and dogs.

For more than six years, she has been teaching workshops at her farm, demonstrating how to prepare various homemade meal plans for cats and dogs. She also does one-on-one consultations with animals and their people, helping guide people in creating meal plans that fit their lifestyle and pet's needs. She often also gives talks to groups of people on pet nutrition and meal planning. She has given nutrition talks at Camp Unleashed as well as at various dog breed and training clubs and pet stores. Her workshops were featured in the *New York Times* in 2011 as well as in *Bark* magazine.

Beyond cats and dogs, she also teaches workshops on organically and naturally raising chickens and other poultry. And she coaches people as well on how to eat and live healthier and more naturally!

When not in the kitchen making pet and people food, she is out on the farm and in the garden growing food. She owns and runs Midsummer Farm in upstate New York, which is USDA–certified organic and offers produce, herbs, cut flowers, plants and seedlings, and eggs. Her eggs are certified by Animal Welfare Approved, one of the strictest certifiers for humane animal treatment.

Index

Boldface references indicate photographs.

A
Alfalfa, 68, 72, 73, 160, 168
Allergies, 7, 13, 18, 28, 43, 47, 60, 85
Amino acids, 20, 56, 73
Anise seed, 68, 168
Antioxidants, 13, 52, 61, 68, 69, 70
Apple Turkey, 131
Arugula, 63
Avocados, 52

B
Baby Shrimp and Carrots, 140
Baked Sweet Potato and Chicken, 126
Baked Sweet Potato and Lamb, 127
Barley and Ground Turkey, 134
Barley and Jack Mackerel, 134
B-complex supplement, 72
Beans, 59
Beef, 18, 36, 46–47
Beef, Sardines, and Polenta, 100
Beef and Veggie Patties, 101
Beef Chunks with Chicken Necks and Eggs, 112
Beef Chunks with Nuts and Seeds, 110, **111**
Beef hearts, 56
Beef marrow or leg bones, 161
Beef Strips Stir-Fry, 151
Big Baked Veggies and Lamb Chunks, 115
Big Baked Veggies and Raw Chicken, 118
Big Baked Veggies and Sautéed Chicken Thighs, 138, **139**
Big Baked Veggies and Soft-Boiled Eggs, 114
Bonemeal, 53
Bones, 39, 40, 47, 50, 53, 55, 73, 161
Breed, personalized meals and, 35
Bright Celery and Cucumber Meal, 116, **117**
Butter, 46, 47, 65

C
Calcium, 53, 55, 63, 73, 75, 87
Canned Fish Trio and Baked Winter Squash with Millet, 145
Carbohydrates, 31, 42
Carnivores, 10, 22, 23, 50, 82, 83
Carob, 55, 168
Carrots, 62, 160, 168
Cheese, 65, 160
Chicken, 18, 28
Chicken and Baked Winter Squash with Organ Meats, 124
Chicken Breasts with Cauliflower and Parsnips, 143
Chicken hearts, 56
Chicken Neck and Turkey Dinner with Seasonal Vegetables, 92
Chicken necks, 42, 47, 55, 80, 88
Chicken Stock, **104**, 105–6

Chicken Thigh Stir-Fry, 152, **153**
Chocolate, avoiding, 74
Coconut and Turmeric Biscuits, 166
Coconut oil, 52
Commercial pet food
    combining homemade food with, 41–42
    drawbacks of, 9, 13, 17, 74, 85
    high-quality, 170–71
    ingredients in, 47, 60
    transitioning from, 30, 33, 40, 85
    universal design of, 27
Cooked Chicken Livers with Sardines, 135
Cornmeal-Chicken Muffins, 162

D
Dairy products, 10, 19, 23, 65, 73, 74
Dark, leafy greens, 63, 73, 87
Diarrhea, 23, 29, 43, 65, 85
Digestive enzymes, 40, 73
Digestive systems, animal, 10, 20, 23, 39, 59, 82
Dill and Dulse Crackers, 167
Dulse, 55, 69, 169
E
Eating style of pet, 34
Eggs, 19, 56, 58, 72, 73, 74
Eggshells, 55
Energy level of pet, 33
Essential fatty acids, 13, 50. See also Omega-3s; Omega-6s
"Essentials" Dinner, 109
Exercise, 33, 40, 82

F
Fasting, 23, 85
Fats, 13, 46, 47, 50–52, 51, 55, 59, 87
Fennel seed, 68, 168
Fiber, 64
Figgy Biscuits, 165
Fish, 18, 47, 49, 51, 72, 73, 83, 160. See also specific fish
Fish oil supplements, 51
Flaxseed oil, 50
Food background of pet, 31
Food preparation, 14, 19, 79–83
Food processor, 61, 80
Food safety guidelines, 21, 83
Free-feeding, avoiding, 82
Freezing meat, 81
Fruits, 61, 62, 70, 72, 168, 169

G
Garlic, 68, 169
Genetically modified organisms (GMOs), 14, 60, 75
Glucosamine and chondroitin supplement, 40
Goat, 18, 47
Grains, 10, 19, 23, 39, 60, 64, 72, 73, 74, 88, 89, 170

Grapes, avoiding, 75
Greens, 19, 63, 73, 80, 87
Green Sardines, 129
Green Turkey, 131
Grinder, 47, 61, 80, 81, 88
Ground Chicken Dinner with Seasonal Vegetables, 90, **91**
Ground Chicken Necks and Beef Mash with Seasonal
    Vegetables, 93
Ground Chicken with Summer Squash, 120
Ground Frozen Fish Mash with Seasonal Vegetables, 94
Ground Lamb, Jack Mackerel, and Cucumber, 128
Ground Turkey with Arugula, 121
Ground Turkey with Tahini, Cucumber, and Lettuce, 121

H
Hearts, 56, 73, 74
Herb and Spice Healthy Supplement Powder, 69
Herbs, 39, 63, 73, 77, 80, 169
History of pet, 28–29
Homemade pet food
    benefits of, 7, 9, 10, 12, 13, 14
    combining commercial foods and, 41–42
    preparing, 14, 19, 79–83
    transitioning to, 30, 33, 40, 43, 84–85
Honey, 68–69, 169
Hot spots, 7, 75
Hydrogenated fats, 52, 74
Hyperactivity, 31

J
Jack mackerel, 18, 51
Jack Mackerel and Veggies, 128

K
Kelp, 55, 69, 72, 73, 169
Kibble, 7, 20, 40, 171
Kitchen equipment, 80
Kittens, feeding, 38–39

L
Lamb, 18, 47
Lamb and Salmon Patties with Wild Greens, 141
Lamb and Salmon with Sunflower Seed Mash, 130
Lecithin, avoiding, 75
Leftover Poultry, 129
Liver, 56, 74, 161
Liver and Parsley Crescent Biscuits, 163
Love Biscuits, 164

M
Mackerel, 49
Meals
frequency of, 22, 82
personalizing, 28–36, 43
planning, 7, 14, 38–40, 42, 89

sample week of, 24
size of, 22, 37, 88
variety of, 12, 17, 18–19, 22, 27, 89
Mealtime guidelines, 39, 82
Meatloaf, 158, **159**
Meat(s), 46–47, 49, 87. See also specific meats
    allergies to, 18, 47
    for cats and dogs, 10
    certified organic, 14
    in commercial pet foods, 170, 171
    cooked, 20
    fats in, 46, 47, 50, 51
    freezing, 81
    grass-fed, 14, 46, 50, 51, 73, 74
    grinding, 21, 34, 42, 61, 80, 81
    ingredients added to, 53, 58, 60, 64
    for meal variety, 18
    omitting, on fasting days, 23
    portion size of, 88
    raw, 20, 21, 47, 83
    vegetables and, 61, 89
    vitamins in, 72, 73
Meaty Bones Stock, 107–8
Mélange Meals, 89
Metabolism, 10, 30, 33, 34, 35, 82
Minerals, 73
Multivitamin, 20, 73
Mung bean sprouts, 68, 160

N
Nettle Rice, 145
Nutrients
    absorption of, 10, 20
    essential, 72–74, 87
    foods high in, 168–69
    general guidelines for, 17
    in homemade pet food, 13, 14
Nutritional balance, 12, 17, 18, 27, 41–42
Nuts, 59, 64, 72, 73, 80, 87, 168, 169

O
Oatmeal and Eggs, 147
Oatmeal and Fish, 142
Oatmeal and Organ Meats, 133
Oats, veggie, 60
Older pets, feeding, 40, 62
Olive oil, 52
Omega-3s, 46, 49, 50–51, 58, 65, 74
Omega-6s, 50, 74
Omnivores, dogs as, 10
Onions, avoiding, 75
Organic foods, 13, 14, 47, 51, 56, 58, 65, 74
Organ meats, 56, 73, 87

P

Parsley, 63, 69, 77, 169
Personality of pet, 31
Personalizing meals
    considerations in, 28–36
    observing reactions to, 43
Pesticides, avoiding, 14
Phosphorus, 53, 75
Plating food, 81
Polenta, Jack Mackerel, and Scrambled Eggs, 144
Polenta and Chicken, 98
Polenta and Ground Lamb with Cruciferous Vegetables, 133
Polenta and Salmon, 96, **97**
Polenta and Sardines with Zucchini, 144
Pork, 49
Portion size, 22, 37, 88
Poultry, 14, 47. See also Chicken; Turkey
Probiotics, 40, 73
Protein, 12, 18, 19, 28, 31. See also specific protein sources
Pumpkin seeds, 59, 169
Puppies, feeding, 38–39
Pure and Simple Meals, 89
Purple Berry Meat, 122

R

Rabbit, 18, 47, 74
Raisins, avoiding, 75
Recipes, 18, 87–89. See also specific recipe names
Roughage, 64

S

Safety guidelines, 21, 83
Salmon, 18, 20, 46, 47, 49, 51, 55
Sardines, 18, 20, 46, 47, 49, 51, 88
Sardine Salad, 154, **155**
Sardines and Beef with Celery and Cucumber, 120
Sardines and Ground Turkey with Millet, 132
Scrambled Eggs with Broccoli, 150
Scrambled Eggs with Salmon and Apple, 135
Seeds, 59, 68, 72, 73, 80, 168, 169
Separation anxiety, 7, 31
Sesame seeds, 59, 169
Shellfish, 18, 49
Size of pet, personalized meals and, 36
Slippery elm bark, 39
Snacks, 160–67
Soft-Boiled Eggs, Baked Carrots, and Ground Chicken, 113
Soft-Boiled Eggs, Barley, and Salmon, 142
Soft-Boiled Eggs, Steamed Spinach, and Salmon, **136**, 137
Stool, 64, 85
Storage containers, 80, 83
Stress, 28–29, 34, 39, 72, 85
Sunflower Seed Mash, 130
Sunflower seeds, 59, 169

Super foods, species-appropriate, 68–69
Supplements, 40, 51, 55, 72–73, 87
Sweet Rose Chicken, 123

T

Tahini, 59, 169
Taurine, 20, 56
Trace minerals, 73
Treats, 160–67
Tuna, 49
Turkey, 18, 55
Turkey, Pea, and Sweet Potato Frittata, 157
Turkey and Veggie Frittata, 156
Turkey with Coconut Oil and Vegetables, 119
Turkey with Millet, Fennel, and Tahini, 95
Turmeric, 69, 169

U

Ultimate Veggie Oats, The, 102, **103**, **146**
Urinary tract problems, 20, 75, 82

V

Vegetables, 10, 14, 19, 39, 60, 61–62, 64, 70, 72, 74, 80, 81, 83, 87, 89, 168, 169, 170
Veggie Oat and Chicken Dinner, 99
Venison, 18, 47
Vitamins, 14, 40, 72, 73

W

Weight of pet, 24, 33, 37, 40, 88
Wheat bran, 64
Whole foods, 9, 10, 12, 18, 19, 40, 72, 73, 160–61

Y

Yeast, avoiding, 75
Yogurt, 65, 73
Yogurt or Soft Cheese Meal, 140

Z

Zucchini and Eggs, 148, **149**
Zucchini and Pumpkin Seed Mash with Chicken Necks, 125